Praise for *Uncivil Rites*

"*Uncivil Rites* reveals Steven Salaita's deep humanity and integrity. Despite the efforts of the University of Illinois to silence him, Salaita continues to speak out courageously for Palestinian rights. His case is a reminder to us all of the need to defend academic freedom and to protect those who challenge the powerful."
—Glenn Greenwald, author, *No Place to Hide*
and *With Liberty and Justice for Some*

"This book is an important historical document, recounting a courageous academic's effort to stand up to institutional racism at one of America's putative preeminent academic institutions."
—Rula Jebreal-Altschul, author, *Miral*

"This is Steven Salaita at his most brilliant, hilarious, incisive, and moving. *Uncivil Rites* is a deeply personal account of Salaita's year since his firing from the University of Illinois over tweets critical of Israel's assault on Gaza. But it is much more than that. Although I have followed every twist of the case since it began, Salaita's unique vantage point provides crucial parts of the story that have been missing until now. Salaita is capable of startling vulnerability and personal revelation, seamlessly shifting back to perfect scholarly detachment, always hitting exactly the right note as he parries with and demolishes his accusers. This masterful book shows that far from diminishing him, the ordeal inflicted on Salaita has spurred him to produce some of his best writing yet. It is essential reading for all of us who believe we must fight to defend free speech against the encroaching corporatization of every aspect and institution of American life."
—Ali Abunimah, cofounder, *Electronic Intifada*
and author, *The Battle for Justice in Palestine*

"*Uncivil Rites* is Steven Salaita's most important work to date. Using his unjust dismissal from University of Illinois as the backdrop, Salaita exposes the intellectual, moral, and political contradictions of the 21st-century neo-liberal university. He also spotlights the dangers of conflating anti-Zionism with anti-Semitism, resistance with terrorism, and righteous outrage with incivility. This book only reinforces Salaita's well-deserved reputation as one of the most honest, courageous, and incisive scholars of our generation."
—Marc Lamont Hill, Distinguished Professor of African American studies, Morehouse College

"Out of the experience of McCarthyism came a literature of memoir and protest that was too good for the history that produced it. Steven Salaita's *Uncivil Rites* is also too good for the events that produced it. A kind of travelogue of the unbound mind, *Uncivil Rites* offers a palimpsest of Salaita's experiences on the road and his reflections—part literary, part historical, part familial—on the politics and personalities of his firing. 'An autobiographical story that is anything but personal,' it is by turns tender, thoughtful, enraging, and often laugh-out-loud funny. Many books feel like a duty; this was sheer pleasure."
—Corey Robin, professor of political science, Brooklyn College and the CUNY Graduate Center

UNCIVIL RITES

PALESTINE AND THE LIMITS
OF ACADEMIC FREEDOM

Steven Salaita

Haymarket Books
Chicago, Illinois

Published by
Haymarket Books
P.O. Box 180165
Chicago, IL 60618
773-583-7884
www.haymarketbooks.org
info@haymarketbooks.org

ISBN: 978-1-60846-577-4

Trade distribution:
In the US, Consortium Book Sales and Distribution, www.cbsd.com
In Canada, Publishers Group Canada, www.pgcbooks.ca
In the UK, Turnaround Publisher Services, www.turnaround-uk.com
All other countries, Publishers Group Worldwide, www.pgw.com

This book was published with the generous support of Lannan Foundation
and the Wallace Action Fund.

Cover design by Dan Tesser. Cover images of Steven Salaita by Tayarisha Poe.

Printed in Canada by union labor.

Library of Congress Cataloging-in-Publication data is available.

10 9 8 7 6 5 4 3 2 1

For he who ignites

Contents

ACKNOWLEDGMENTS

This book is partly about me, but only as I have been actualized by various communities. Before we proceed, I wish to recognize numerous people who have enabled my intellectual, mental, and moral actualization. I beg of the reader not to harbor any resentment toward these folks for my own shortcomings.

Matthew and Christina Shenoda: your love and wisdom are peerless; Ben and Jenny Sax: thank you for always offering your friendship and your home in moments of trouble (and joy); John and Peter Housein: "in law" does nothing to describe my actual perception of you; Michael Salaita: you demolish all negative connotations of the phrase "big brother"; Danya Lynch: few things make me prouder than calling you my sister; Mom and Dad: you created me—I love you all the more because you're proud to live with the result; my beautiful nieces and nephews: you are each wise beyond my years; Nasri and Delia: I adore being thought of as one of your own; Mohammed Abed: our friendship, like the justice, can never be divided; Ahmed Ghappour: may I ever be on your good side—it's glorious over there; Corey Robin: just wow; Michael Smith and Michael Ratner: you are models of principled dissent; Lisa Kahaleole Hall: puppies and toddlers forever; Ali Abunimah: when we change the world, you'll get that Pulitzer; Robert Warrior: my words can never do you justice; Keeanga-Yamahtta Taylor and Lauryn Fleer: my favorite power couple; Vicente Diaz: please keep fucking with things in an Island way; J. Kehaulani Kauanui: you're one of the few people who could convince me to do acupuncture, and yet I'm not at all surprised that it works; Magid Shihade and Sunaina Maira: I talk often of your fierce intelligence but not enough about your deep kindness; David Lloyd: you are a moral giant; Dina Omar: some streets can be judged by the quality of company rather than the architecture; Salah Hassan: I never fail to learn tons whenever we talk; Junaid Rana: you do not get nearly enough credit for your superb organizing—I hope this shout-out helps; Mimi Nguyen: the same is true of you and your constant badassery; Sarah Roberts: you've been there from the beginning, and nobody doubts you'll stay to the end; Rico Kleinstein Chenyek: *abrazos y solidaridad*; Donna Nevel and Alan Levine: I always carry your kindness; Eman Ghanayem: you are the hero of this story; Stephanie Skora: you are what a real undergraduate educator looks like; Jodi Byrd: the empire will never withstand your fierce intellect; Nadine Naber: I often joke that we're tribesfolk, and I reiterate it here—this time, though, it has nothing to do with nationality or geography; David Palumbo-Liu: your energy and effervescence constantly inspire; Jasbir Puar: so many rely on your fierce compassion; Evelyn Alsultany: you are our model of probity.

Nobody knows how to campaign with integrity, intelligence, and efficiency like the members of the USACBI Organizing Collective, a body of which I'm grateful to be a member. Individually, you are each brilliant; collectively, you are a lifeline.

SJP, SAIA, SUPER, and SPHR: please keep teaching everybody how principled activism should be conducted.

This country would be much worse without the Center for Constitutional Rights, particularly the splendid Baher Azmy, Maria LaHood, and Omar Shakir.

Anand Swaminathan, Jon Loevy, and Gretchen Helfrich of Loevy and Loevy in Chicago have handled my legal case with dignity, empathy, and intelligence.

I would love to take credit for the wonderful phrase "uncivil rites," but credit goes to the great Elyse Crystall, who used it as the title of an event she organized for me at UNC–Chapel Hill.

The team at Haymarket, particularly the preternaturally patient Anthony Arnove, has been a joy to work with. Ruth Baldwin and Dao Tran are terrific editors.

And Diana: a less loving spouse might have found hundreds of reasons to give up on me. Even difficult situations offer life in its greatest incarnation as long as we have cause to be together. Thank you for the strength and persistence. I love you.

INTRODUCTION

In August 2014, I was fired from a tenured position in the American Indian Studies Program at the University of Illinois at Urbana-Champaign (UIUC). Contrary to the university's expectations, the firing made me something of a free speech darling (or the world's most violent person since Stalin) and caused serious damage to UIUC's reputation (and, by virtue of the university's statements, my own).[1] As I write this, exactly nine months since the termination, the debate around matters of academic freedom, faculty governance, the Israel-Palestine conflict, and the role of social media in university life rages with no resolution in sight. The University of Illinois and Salaita are now practically synonymous.

Our synonymity began with a run-of-the-mill job application. The American Indian Studies Program sought somebody doing comparative work in global Indigenous Studies. For me it was a culmination of an unorthodox career. I majored in political science as an undergraduate and immediately after graduation pursued an MA in English. While completing the degree I took a course in the Native American novel and became addicted to all things Indigenous, writing a thesis on interrelated discourses of colonization in North America and Palestine, the basis on which I completed my

---

1. Chairman of the Board of Trustees Christopher Kennedy called the public response "super surprising."

1

doctorate in Native American Studies at the University of Oklahoma in 2003. A few years after graduation I published my dissertation as *The Holy Land in Transit: Colonialism and the Quest for Canaan*, and followed it up with five more books on topics ranging from modern Arab American fiction to the pratfalls of liberal piety.

I took a tenure-track job directly out of grad school at the University of Wisconsin-Whitewater (UWW); I stayed at UWW for three years before accepting a position in English at Virginia Tech, where I earned tenure in 2009. During my eight years at Tech, I created a variety of courses in Native Studies, critical theory, ethnicity, and global literature. I became a regular columnist at various online publications—*The Electronic Intifada*, *Salon*, *MondoWeiss*, and so forth—usually in relation to Palestine, though also on a variety of topics of interest to a leftist audience. I joined the organizing collective of the US Campaign for the Academic and Cultural Boycott of Israel (USACBI) and advocated for Boycott, Divestment, and Sanctions (BDS). These final two biographical notes—writing for public consumption and organizing around Palestine—foreground my troubles with UIUC because outing oneself as pro-Palestine is a troublesome prospect in academe.

Uncivil Rites presents a series of essays both personal and analytical. Since my employment termination, I wrote whenever I could find the time: in the frenzied moments before boarding an airplane; late at night in hotel rooms, the uncomforting noise of *SportsCenter* in the background; between meetings with graduate students and radio hosts; on rickety Amtrak trains, fighting the need to sleep; in coffee shops with unreliable Wi-Fi; and after the exhaustive work of reviewing legal documents. From these sporadic doodles a book emerged. The meaning of "book" becomes less clear by the month. I still think of the book primarily as a physical object, which proffers me serious Luddite credentials I would prefer to avoid. A book, like a music album, is no longer a self-contained document or, in more exciting moments, a cultural event. It can be a file, or hypertext, or a self-published pamphlet (meaning a PDF file, not quite the same item that Thomas Paine produced). In whatever manifestation, the book as we conceptualize it must now be seen as more than merely an organized textual object. The one you now read serves as a culmination of a demand to quit revising and finally commit to production.

The essay is no easier to define. In the days of blogging, tweeting, editorializing, testimonials, product reviews, Facebook notes, and selfies, not even Montaigne could have foreseen the genre's mutations. I am no troglodyte nostalgic for the days of pitch-perfect pieces published in snooty journals as artifacts of cultured elegance. I welcome the new ways of producing and sharing text that are constantly discovered by creative (and—let's be fair—sometimes tedious) consumers of culture. It has become impossible for me to consider nonfiction a hermetic enterprise. Attempting to explain the simulacra of hypertextual branding usually results in their reproduction.

In the aftermath of the controversy with UIUC, I spent nine months constantly on the road, speaking before large crowds or chatting with audiences of two, depending on the time and place. It was an instructive period, something I could never have imagined before it happened and have no desire to repeat. Traveling is a young man's pursuit. I don't know exactly when I eclipsed the mythical realm of "youthful," but surely it occurred before I became a parent and assumed bougie habits like paying a mortgage and taking regular showers.[2] Audiences were receptive, though I encountered plenty of disagreement with my anti-Zionist points of view—just not enough to disturb my belief that Zionism is waning in power on campus. I discussed my firing and scholarship and the relationship of both to various phenomena of concern to activists and academics, talking myself hoarse in weeklong, regional increments.

I missed much of my son's third year and left my spouse to

---

2. That I do either of these things consistently is a matter of debate.

handle a two-hour commute and omnipresent familial pressure. We had spent much time considering these outcomes before deciding that I should accept speaking invitations, but no amount of talk prepares the imagination for reality. In many ways, *Uncivil Rites* is a chronicle of these experiences: so many of my observations and discoveries arose from friendly feedback and hostile remonstration, the latter a reliable indicator of consciousness about Palestine in the United States. I met students, scholars, and organizers whose ideas fiercely upend moral and methodological commonplaces. If I could convey a single point about the experience of being fired and ending up as a news story, it would be that oppressive institutions can never subdue the agility of mind and spirit. Humans can be disciplined, but humanity comprises a tremendous antidisciplinary force.

Uncivil Rites is, in every way I have attempted to imagine it, a communal project. It's a book about text that can't be contained on paper. It's a deliberate act of spontaneity. It tells an autobiographical story that is anything but personal.

ONE

Tweet Tweet

Does Twitter lend itself to civility? What ethical responsibilities pertain to users of the platform? Is it a good idea for scholars to tweet? Is it even appropriate?

These questions are difficult to answer without concomitant analysis of the medium and the conditions of public discourse in general. Rhetoric arises in a context. In fact, it is context that allows us to identify an act of rhetoric in the first place. It is foolish to treat a tweet as if it is an aphorism (or, for that matter, to treat an aphorism as if it's merely aphoristic). Twitter entails its own etiquette, which, like the platform from which it emerged, is dynamic and contested. Different users have disparate understandings of that etiquette. They also have different uses for the platform itself.

I use Twitter (though at a much lesser rate these days) as a form of news gathering. I follow a large number of users, the vast majority sharing my interests, so in just a few minutes I can find tons of information and commentary from both corporate and alternative sources. Twitter is an excellent aggregator. One can customize her news intake by carefully choosing whom to follow (and by making use of the "block" button).

I also use it to comment on various sociopolitical phenomena, though Palestine is my most frequent subject. Beyond Palestine, I put forward a decolonial perspective that draws from certain influences, among them Indigenous thought, critical theory, and literary analysis. It's difficult to impart observations without direct reference to those influences, but that's what I try to do. Most of my tweets distill decolonial theory into workaday language. Tweets are not scholarship, however. Academics can express things on Twitter (or other social media) that are verboten in peer-reviewed journals.

I cuss sometimes because why the fuck not? I consider it deeply embarrassing (for them) that some of my colleagues sermonized about my foul mouth. It's a type of moralism that doesn't even rise to the level of disingenuous. It is also profoundly anti-intellectual. All languages have cuss words. They're necessary to human communication. That's why people who don't cuss technically still cuss functionally, by replacing verboten words with their benign equivalent (*goshdarnit, shoot, dang it, flying flip, dookie, bullspit, dagnabbit, doo-doo, son of a biscuit eater*, and my favorite, *mickey-fickey*). Sure, cuss words can be abused and they can be used imprudently. I'm open to the critique that I've made both mistakes. Still, it's nothing to get fired over.

Finally, I use Twitter to share news of both the world and of me. I post articles I imagine will be of interest to followers. I plug friends' work. I tell silly jokes. I offer cooking tips. And, let's be honest, there's a self-promotional aspect to the platform. Scholars are in want of readers; when one's statement is "faved" or retweeted, it offers a concrete sense of engagement. I can distribute my articles and news of talks and travels to a decent-sized audience. The word "audience" is pivotal: Twitter provides access to communities many academics (I included) might otherwise not generate. Those audiences are variable; their investment in the platform tenuous, but users can at least perceive their presence. The imaginary of Twitter is much easier to comprehend than its reality.

(I also enjoy the bickering that frequently occurs among users. Some of the bickering is intensely clever; in other cases it's crude or debauched. Please don't judge me: it's helped me break my addiction to reality TV and pro wrestling. Besides, any decent shrink can tell you that schadenfreude is highly therapeutic.)

I don't find arguments about the limitations of 140 characters to be convincing. Obviously, having only 140 characters limits our capacity to yammer or contextualize, but that limitation enacts creativity in other ways. Like any other medium, sometimes Twitter is an effective site of conversation; at other times it is inadequate. Neither instance provides an excuse to suspend reading comprehension.

Reading closely and carefully is a tremendous asset to political consciousness. It allows us to discern the nuance inherent to statements of belief, even when nuance is unintended. Great things have been said in less than 140 characters. For example:

- "I have never let my schooling interfere with my education."—Mark Twain
- "We didn't land on Plymouth Rock, Plymouth Rock landed on us."—Malcolm X
- "We ask for nothing that is not right, and herein lies the great power of our demand."—Paul Robeson
- "Where there is occupation there is resistance. This is basic, it's natural; you cannot change the sun and make it rise from the west."—Leila Khaled
- "Of the love or hatred God has for the English, I know nothing, but I know that they will be thrown out of France, except those who die there."—Joan of Arc
- "Love is or it ain't. Thin love ain't love at all."—Toni Morrison
- "Poverty is the worst form of violence."—Gandhi
- "There is no necessity to separate the monarch from the mob; all authority is equally bad."—Oscar Wilde

- "Chance has never yet satisfied the hope of a suffering people."—Marcus Garvey
- "The white man knows how to make everything, but he does not know how to distribute it."—Sitting Bull
- "No pen can give an adequate description of the all-pervading corruption produced by slavery." —Harriet Ann Jacobs (Linda Brent)
- "I may not be a smart man, but I know what love is." —Forrest Gump

It is apocryphal to suggest that Twitter cannot accommodate critical or comprehensive thought. I'd take Sitting Bull's observation, for instance, over all sixty-five editions of *Freakonomics*. It's true that countless stupid things have been said in 140 characters, but this is less a problem of medium than of stupidity. Serious analysis can, and should, occur on the platform.

As to the tweets that put me in so much trouble, I can best explain them by quoting passages from my feed that the UIUC administration and its supporters assiduously ignored:

- May 11, 2014: #MyMomTaughtMe that politics without empathy results in politicians.
- July 17, 2014: I absolutely have empathy for Israeli civilians who are harmed. Because I'm capable of empathy, I deeply oppose colonization and ethnocracy.
- July 18, 2014: It's a beautiful thing to see our Jewish brothers and sisters around the world deploring #Israel's brutality in #Gaza.
- July 19, 2014: If it's "anti-Semitic" to deplore colonization, land theft, and child murder, then what choice does any person of conscience have? #Gaza
- July 19, 2014: My stand is fundamentally one of acknowledging and countering the horror of antisemitism.
- July 22, 2014: Those said to be expressing anger are in real-

ity often articulating love for fellow humans who are suffering. #Gaza #FreePalestine

- July 23, 2014: #ISupportGaza because I believe that Jewish and Arab children are equal in the eyes of God.
- July 27, 2014: I refuse to conceptualize #Israel/#Palestine as Jewish-Arab acrimony. I am in solidarity with many Jews and in disagreement with many Arabs.
- July 28, 2014: The first thing colonization asks of its beneficiaries is to suppress their capacity for empathy. #Gaza #Israel
- July 29, 2014: Yes, some seek vengeance. Others seek come-uppance. Most of us, however, only ask for simple human compassion. #Gaza #Israel

These ruminations offer a representative sampling of my Twitter feed. Judge that feed as you wish. If you are being honest, however, you cannot judge it as violent or anti-Semitic (unless you define anti-Semitism as criticism of the Israeli state). If you decide anyway to judge it as violent, then I hope you might at least acknowledge that the word "violence" isn't neutral. If you are incapable of such an acknowledgment, then consider yourself perfectly suited for a career in campus middle management.

As to my apparent hatred of Jews, let's clarify: I never called anti-Semitism honorable; I called "antisemitism" honorable. The scare quotes represent a critical shift of meaning. They indicate displeasure with ersatz principle presented in the guise of pious liberal policing. The many tweets framing the comment also make it indisputably clear that I'm critiquing a discourse rather than endorsing any sort of racism. The controversial tweet draws from a longstanding conversation about the discursive uses of "anti-Semitism" in debates around the Israel-Palestine conflict. Again, I don't expect everybody to agree with me. I only request that they respond to the argument I raised and not to the phantom outrage of right-wing operatives.

Because this debacle emerged from the machinations of right-wing operatives, I see no need to offer an exegesis of my controversial tweets (which don't even number in the double digits). On July 21, 2014, the *Daily Caller*, Tucker Carlson's[3] online enterprise, ran a piece about me titled "University of Illinois Professor Blames Jews for Anti-Semitism." With the brio and wisdom for which far-right websites are known, the piece begins, "The University of Illinois at Urbana-Champaign has continued its bizarre quest to employ as many disgusting scumbags as possible by acquiring the services of Steven Salaita, a leading light in the movement among similarly obscure academics to boycott Israel."

Please remember the origin of my firing whenever academics sermonize the importance of objective standards in hiring decisions. Also remember that nobody cares more about the Jewish people than Christian Zionists and Tucker Carlson.

There is one tweet I'd like to explain, though, for it's received much attention and illuminates relevant issues: "You may be too refined to say it, but I'm not: I wish all the fucking West Bank settlers would go missing." I sent the tweet on June 19, 2014, less than two weeks after the disappearance of three Israeli teenagers and eleven days before they were found buried in a shallow grave near Khalil (Hebron). The Israeli government immediately blamed Hamas, which turned out not to be responsible, and facilitated one of the worst outbreaks of mob violence in recent Israeli history, replete with racial hysteria and genocidal desire.[4]

The teenagers lived in a settlement. During the period of their

---

3. He has a shaggy mop of chestnut hair. He wears a bowtie. He is white. His name is Tucker. Clearly he was created in a Republican lab.
4. Mordechai Kedar, lecturer in Arabic literature at Bar-Ilan University, had this to say: "The only thing that can deter terrorists like those who kidnapped the children and killed them is the knowledge that their sister or their mother will be raped. It sounds very bad, but that's the Middle East. I'm not talking about what we should or shouldn't do. I'm talking about the facts." Added IDF major general Oren Shachor, "If we kill their families, that will frighten them."

absence, the phrase "gone missing" or "go missing" was in wide circulation. I thought it a suitable moment to reflect on a fundamental Palestinian desire to end military occupation. I invoked the "go missing" phrase because of its currency in that moment. I didn't mean kidnap or murder. Had I desired either of these outcomes, I would have used the terms appropriate to that desire. At this point of my life, I've shared more than ten thousand tweets, published six books and many scholarly articles, and written dozens of essays. Nowhere in that body of work do I endorse abduction or murder. If folks want to weigh one tweet whose meaning is unclear against a career-spanning sample size, then it would help their case if they could find at least one more thing I've said that endorses or implies violent commitments. We also need to consider that the tweet was interpreted in the worst possible light by people who had targeted me for recrimination long before I ever composed it.

We can slosh around forever in interpretations that amount to an intentional fallacy, but I've stated my reasoning and there's not much more I can add to assuage those who find the tweet disturbing. Yet there's analytic potential in both the tweet and the responses it inspired.

I submit that the hysteria the tweet generated was less about an ostensible incitement to violence and more about the profound anxieties of colonial self-esteem. Israelis want to be accepted by Palestinians, even loved. No state frets more about its image among its enemies or speaks so openly about the need for its neighbors' acceptance. Few things are as frustrating as an oppressor who demands adoration. My tweet, in its ambivalent crudeness, rejects that possibility. The recalcitrance of the native has always been a psychological blow to colonizers.

I understand why those who mythologize Israel as benign don't want to hear it and why they don't like to hear it, but hear it they must, even if they refuse to listen: Palestinians don't like settlers.

They don't want settlers in their ancestral land. They want the set-tlers gone, to go missing if you will. It's a normal reaction to the continual pain and suffering the settlers inflict.

There are nearly half a million Jewish settlers on the West Bank. Their population currently grows at double the rate of other Israelis. They use 90 percent of the West Bank's water; the 3.5 million Pal-estinians of the territory make do with the remaining 10 percent. They travel on Jewish-only highways while Palestinians wait for hours at checkpoints (with no guarantee of passing through, even when they are injured or giving birth). They regularly assault wom-en and children; some bury alive the natives. They vandalize homes and shops. They run over pedestrians with their cars. They restrict farmers from their land. They squat on hilltops that don't belong to them. They firebomb houses and kill babies. They bring with them a high-tech security force largely composed of conscripts to maintain this hideous apparatus. As of this writing, Israel's illegal settlement of the West Bank continues unabated.

No native population accepts foreign settlement. This is such a self-evident point as to almost be a truism, and yet the settlers' disquiet continues to define normative discourse in academe. When Natives of the upper plains adopted the Ghost Dance in the late nineteenth century, white settlers reacted harshly to its prescription that they disappear, though the dance entailed much more. Its pop-ularity contributed to the conditions that led to the 1890 Wounded Knee massacre. Gandhi implored followers to pray for the expul-sion of the British. In the modern United States, the notion of "re-verse racism" is a byproduct of settler colonial anxiety.

Frantz Fanon wrote in 1963:

> The zone where the natives live is not complementary to the zone inhabited by the settlers. The two zones are opposed, but not in the service of a higher unity.
>   No conciliation is possible, for of the two terms, one is su-

perfluous. The settlers' town is a strongly-built town, all made of stone and steel. It is a brightly-lit town; the streets are covered with asphalt, and the garbage-cans swallow all the leavings, unseen, unknown and hardly thought about. The settler's feet are never visible, except perhaps in the sea; but there you're never close enough to see them. His feet are protected by strong shoes although the streets of his town are clean and even, with no holes or stones. The settler's town is a well-fed town, an easy-going town; its belly is always full of good things. The settler's town is a town of white people, of foreigners.

The town belonging to the colonised people, or at least the native town, the negro village, the medina, the reservation, is a place of ill fame, peopled by men of evil repute. They are born there, it matters little where or how; they die there, it matters not where, nor how. It is a world without spaciousness; men live there on top of each other, and their huts are built one on top of the other. The native town is a hungry town, starved of bread, of meat, of shoes, of coal, of light. The native town is a crouching village, a town on its knees, a town wallowing in the mire. It is a town of niggers and dirty Arabs. The look that the native turns on the settler's town is a look of lust, a look of envy; it expresses his dreams of possession, all manner of possession: to sit at the settler's table, to sleep in the settler's bed, with his wife if possible. The colonised man is an envious man. And this the settler knows very well; when their glances meet he ascertains bitterly, always on the defensive "They want to take our place." It is true, for there is no native who does not dream at least once a day of setting himself up in the settler's place.

I have yet to meet a Palestinian who tells me the "go missing" tweet was inappropriate. (Doubtless that person exists, but he appears to be gravely outnumbered.) After all, removed from the constraints of colonial logic, the sentiment makes perfect sense.

In the hegemon, state violence is never violent. Expressions of the subaltern, however, are always said to be conducted violently. Indicting a lone tweeter allows those invested in the colonial apparatus to avoid confronting their own complicity in the cruelties of racism and war. Many folks wrung their hands—teeth gnashed into rugged nubs—about my tweets critical of Israel while saying nothing of Israel's wanton slaughter in Gaza. If, in the imagination of the liberal state, racism is but an individual failing, then critique of structural violence is a collective evasion.

During the summer of 2014, in fifty-one days, as part of Operation Protective Edge, Israel left Gaza a pile of rubble. In the following months we learned more about the horror. Gaza lacked water and electrical infrastructure. Most residents experienced eighteen-hour blackouts.[5] Without adequate electricity, water treatment plants couldn't properly function. Pools of sewage collected in some neighborhoods. Garbage couldn't be regularly collected. Israel destroyed dozens of boats, leaving numerous fishermen without work. Many schools were unusable. Israel flattened thousands of buildings. Gazans experienced more than $5 billion in property damage. In many cases they used mud to reconstruct their properties. A decade-old travel ban remained in place.

During the slaughter, by which point Palestinians had killed two Israeli Jews, Binyamin Netanyahu proclaimed, "[The invasion] was justified. It was proportional." Former defense minister and current head of the Knesset's Foreign Affairs and Defense Committee Avigdor Lieberman added, "We need to return to the Gaza Strip and conduct a thorough cleaning," noting, when asked about the scenes of terrible destruction, "Our soldiers did a good job." Israel's minister of the economy, Naftali Bennett, rehashed neoconservative clichés circa 2001: "For the free world to win, we need to start by realizing one simple thing—no matter what the name of the organization, the enemy is the same. It might be called Hezbollah in Lebanon, ISIS in Iraq, Hamas in the Gaza Strip and Al-Nusra in Syria. All have the same goal—to attack the Western democratic way of life wherever it might be."[6]

---

5. Israel shelled Gaza's only power plant on July 29, 2014.
6. Bennett's invocation of the Nusra Front is notable considering the evidence of

Israeli leaders have a long history of racist pronouncements, particularly around matters of demography. Early Zionist leaders were intent on creating and then maintaining a Jewish majority in Palestine. David Ben-Gurion (née Green) observed, "A Jewish majority is not Zionism's last station, but it is a very important station on the route to Zionism's political triumph. It will give our security and presence a sound foundation, and allow us to concentrate masses of Jews in this country and the region." He also noted that "the Arab must not and cannot be a Zionist. He could never wish the Jews to become a majority. This is the true antagonism between us and the Arabs. We both want to be the majority." Ben-Gurion was realistic. In attributing normal desires for freedom to Arabs, he fundamentally accepted them as human. At the same time, he was acutely aware of the inconvenience those feelings might cause the nascent Jewish state. In demanding a Jewish majority, Ben-Gurion allowed the racism of European social engineering to overcome his humanistic instinct.

This tradition continues, but with much less intelligence. Having declared that "Israel is a Jewish state, and I want to stress that our nation is the Jewish nation," in 2008 centrist (Kadima) leader Tzipi Livni proposed a plan of forced transfer of Palestinian citizens of Israel. Lieberman proposed a more specific transfer plan six years later. MK (Minister of Knesset) Ayelet Shaked called Palestinians "little snakes" and asserted that "the entire Palestinian people is the enemy."[7] She continued: "In wars the enemy is usually an entire people, including its elderly and its women, its cities and its villages, its property and its infrastructure." Bennett once bragged, "I have killed lots of Arabs in my life—and there is no problem with that." In 2013, the mayor of Nazareth Illit (Upper Nazareth), Shimon Gafsou, ran a reelection campaign on the slogan "Nazareth Illit Jewish Forever." One billboard proclaimed: "No more accepting the

---

the group's collaboration with Israel.
7. Shaked was later rewarded with appointment as Israel's justice minister.

law that makes possible [*sic*] for every citizen to live where he wants. It's time to guard the home." Gafsou, under various corruption indictments, won the election. He at least had the decency to embrace his identity as "racist scum," a confession he predicted (correctly) would comfort his supporters. It's worth a mention that Nazareth Illit can be described as an internal settlement, as opposed to Nazareth proper, an Arab village for many centuries.

Such racism extends to African migrants in Israel, as when Likud MK Miri Regev referred to them as a "cancer on our body" in 2013. Interior Minister Gideon Sa'ar was more diplomatic: "There are currently around 30 million people moving around Africa, people who have left their home countries and are looking for a place to be. We can all understand that pressure, but if we are too liberal, then we will lose the country. We will lose the only Jewish country that exists." While African migrants were facing mob violence and concentration camps, an Israeli Defense Force (IDF) poll found that more than half of Israelis agreed with Regev's characterization of them as a cancer. The notion of the state as a body inhabited only by the chosen highlights the psychology of racial purity underlying the settler's ethnocratic imperatives. The non-Jew is cancerous because it upsets a corporeal equilibrium and must be expunged through a cleansing of carnal impurities. The African, like the Arab, is but a mass of unwelcome malignancy.

Given this long history of racist comment—by mainstream politicians, mind you, not fringe groups—it is reasonable to ascribe genocidal intent to the Israeli government when it bombards nearly two million non-Jews entrapped in a space twice the size of Washington, DC. It's difficult to conceptualize the violence as reluctant or defensive when leaders of that government repeatedly speak in biblical overtones of bloodlust and retribution. I would humbly suggest to Israel's supporters that if they don't like interpretations of the state's violence that treat it as systemic, then they ought to muzzle the dozens of politicians who declare that abusing Arabs and Africans is central to Israel's political system.

Arguments about Hamas rockets and reprisals and cycles of violence have limited use. First of all, it's difficult to ascertain the conditions under which one side in any given moment can be said to have "started it." (Don't misread my point: Israel has clearly broken plenty of ceasefires through the years.) More important, skirmishes and clashes exist within a paradigm of colonization. Analyses that follow this pattern often imply an equivalence of both power and motive. I wouldn't argue that all Palestinian resistance is ethical or prudent, but it's important to remember that it's the violence (and often nonviolence) of the colonized party. Moral and legal frameworks underline this reality. Israel, on the other hand, is the colonial power. As such, its mere presence is an act of violence.

Who (or what) started it? It's quite simple. The answer never changes: the Zionist colonization of Palestine started it. Only the decolonization of Palestine will end it.

Even if we limit ourselves to contexts of equivalence, Israel gets the worst of it. Since 2000, Israelis have killed 2,060 Palestinian children while Palestinians have killed 130 Israeli children. The overall death count during this period is over 9,000 Palestinians and 1,190 Israelis. Israel has violated at least seventy-seven UN resolutions and numerous provisions of the Fourth Geneva Conventions. Israel has imposed hundreds of settlements on the West Bank, while Palestinians inside Israel increasingly are squeezed and continue to be internally displaced. Israel has demolished nearly thirty thousand Palestinian homes as a matter of policy. Palestinians have demolished zero Israeli homes. At present, more than six thousand Palestinians languish in Israeli prisons, including children; no Israeli occupies a Palestinian prison.

Those who fret about the tone of my tweets needn't bother. Nobody asked sanctimonious paladins of colonial society to intervene and impart to the subaltern their wisdom. We have a language with which we speak of Israel. To accommodate normative sensibilities is to forfeit the only power we have over the colonizer: the ability to reject its rapacious demands and, in so doing, its very existence.

TWO

Palestine, (un)Naturally

The geography is dry and withered, humid and verdant, rugged and restful—a cacophony, but also an ensemble. It is a panorama of glorious, incessant contradiction. But not everybody can see it. For many, it is a simulation of ideology, a diversion into mythic cultural adventure, an insatiable geopolitical headache, an inaccessible aspiration, or an unsolved mystery. For the apostate and pious alike, it is always in some way holy. It will never be decolonized unless it is first demythologized. Settlement and myth are symbiotic.

Despite its continuous reinvention, we can still speak of Palestine as an actual place, with geologic formations and a climate classification and an observable ecosystem. Those phenomena undergo actual change. Humans physically experience their alteration. Flora live and die by them. Fauna migrate and immigrate to unnatural places.

The cultural history of Palestine's landscape is also observable. I've heard many Palestinians note the visual similarities between their homeland and Los Angeles. Those similarities aren't an accident. Palm trees are ubiquitous to LA, but none of them is indigenous to the city's territory. They are an import from Mexico and North Africa to coastal Southern California. Early settlers wanted to brand the region. (It explains a lot about the modern city, doesn't it?) Conceptualizing dry, temperate Los Angeles as a tropical paradise proved far-fetched, so they concocted a Mediterranean theme.

Many settlers were Spaniards with a religious mandate, so a Holy Land symbology emerged. This entailed palm trees, which inform important biblical events, including the story of Jesus's birth. The trees also create a visual orientation in scriptural themes. Images of Palestine (real and imagined) have also influenced literature, music, painting, fashion, architecture, and landscaping. Such images have likewise inspired conquest and colonization.

This is all to say that Palestine's natural history is also profoundly artificial.

I have no ability to describe Palestine without yet again performing a reinvention, which makes the landscape so magical. I am convinced it has something to do with the difficulties of its political existence. On second thought, perhaps it has everything to do with them.

We can understand the entirety of the Israel-Palestine conflict by examining its physical effect on the land. The availability of space for human habitation illuminates the hardships of Israeli colonization. (Human habitation partners with military occupation to destroy the environment.) Where do Palestinians live? Maps show us the incongruous geographies of areas A, B, and C, but only life on the ground properly conveys Palestine's fragmentation.

We needn't contemplate where Palestinians live, then. It's better to ask, "Where *can* they live?" The legal restrictions on their habitation are well known, but the spatial limitations of their existence are more conspicuous. Israeli settlement consumes land and thus restricts space. It requires highways and walls and military installations. The West Bank is a bit smaller than Delaware. The portions of it under nominal Palestinian control could fit inside Jacksonville's city limits. Though it doesn't physically disappear, Palestine is forever shrinking.

Even where Palestinians reside, their inhabitance is never secure. Israel demolishes homes, seizes farmland, rezones cities, clean-cuts forests, flattens hilltops, and erects concrete monstrosities within and around villages. Nevertheless, the Palestinian does not populate inorganic structures, but a luminous, living history. No bulldozer can destroy memory.

Memory enables Palestine to survive despite its persistent destruction. Israel has stolen millions of dunums of Palestinian land, with no sign of abatement. (The verb "appropriate" is more diplomatic, but I reckon we ought to use blunt words to describe ugly actions.) In 2014, the Netanyahu government claimed more than a thousand acres of the West Bank for settlement expansion. The number of Jewish settlers creeps toward half a million. Israel siphons water and returns it to Palestinians in the form of sewage. It builds with no regard for the influence of human activity on the land.

Inside Israel, Palestinians are similarly restricted. Israel contorts geography for the sake of demographic expediency, preventing the reestablishment of depopulated villages and locating new developments in places that will ensure Jewish expansion while retarding the growth of Muslim and Christian communities. Nazareth Illit is one example. Built on the hills overlooking the ancient Palestinian city, most famous as the home of Mary and Joseph, Nazareth Illit—Upper Nazareth—exemplifies Israel's desire for ethnocentric jurisdiction. Upper Nazareth, as its lofty name implies, seeks to recreate the city by mythologizing disappearance as an ancient reclamation project.

Thirteen percent of Palestine belongs to the Jewish National Fund (JNF), which has desired to refurbish the Holy Land since 1901. The JNF facilitates development, plants trees, sponsors public works, and manages parkland. The primary effect of its work has been to transform Palestine into an Orientalized theme park, open only to those of a certain ethnic background. It all makes more sense if we think of Israeli settlement as a form of geostrategic gentrification.

We can't properly understand Israel's most recent land grab without discussing what preceded it. Operation Protective Edge, Israel's fifty-one-day siege of the Gaza Strip in the summer of 2014, left the territory in shambles. Gaza's modern natural history can be summed up by its role as clearinghouse for nearly two million non-Jews disallowed in Israel. Shortly after wrecking the Gaza Strip, leaving its population to suffer the fallout of structural and economic collapse, Israel announced its new settlement plans on the West Bank.

Israel has performed this strategy often enough for it to have become predictable: bomb Gaza, steal the West Bank. There is a horrifying logic to its colonial violence.

Still Palestine endures. Its Indigenes recall the landscape that sustained our ancestors and gave rise to our existence, in many cases a continent away. Palestine endures in the way we select olives from the grocery store; plant fig and citrus trees in our backyards; decry the mischaracterization of our cuisine; display pictures of Jerusalem; affix images of Handala to protest signs; and revive our forebears in the naming of children.

There's a certain way to show that Israelis are fundamentally outsiders to the land, but, unfortunately, it doesn't much resonate in the United States, in no small part because Americans are fundamentally outsiders to the land they occupy, as well. I speak of olive trees, which exemplify the phrase "labor of love." The trees take years to bear fruit. Once they do, though, they can provide for centuries. The curved, cragged trees, blending into the tawny environs of surrounding earth, are ubiquitous throughout the West Bank and the Galilee, often arranged in captivating symmetry. Nearly every Palestinian I know owns some type of olivewood icon.

Since 1967, Israel has bulldozed more than 800,000 olive trees. Settlers routinely destroy orchards, having uprooted more than 11,000 olive trees last year alone. Government officials cite practical reasons for the destruction, all of them involving the apocryphal word "security." Much of the time, however, they are simply being punitive.

A Palestinian would never destroy a healthy olive tree. This reality clarifies the so-called complexities of the Israel-Palestine conflict. Who is Indigenous, Jews or Palestinians? A Palestinian would never destroy a healthy olive tree. Who is the aggressor? A Palestinian would never destroy a healthy olive tree. Who has a deep history on the land? A Palestinian would never destroy a healthy olive tree. Who wrecks the environment with irresponsible human settlement? A Palestinian would never destroy a healthy olive tree.

Even if it is incomprehensible to capitalists, politicians, and much of the American public, it is the correct answer to any inquiry about instigations of violence: a Palestinian would never destroy a healthy olive tree.

૨✒

There are feral dogs on the West Bank. They outnumber hyenas, which may not be extinct but are mostly the stuff of legend. The Anatolian leopard, a character in the Bible and the *Epic of Gilgamesh*, is elusive and exhausted. Animals don't recognize human borders. When we build fences between jurisdictions, we inhibit migratory patterns and mating rituals. When we use supposedly empty places to test weaponry, we degrade food and water sources through chemical pollution. When we move people into new places for the purpose of demographic engineering, we also affect the tenuous existence of flora and fauna.

I know about Palestine's feral dogs from experience. I studied for a summer at Birzeit University, near Ramallah, in 2000. I remember the year well because soon upon return to my US doctoral institution, the second Intifada began. I was a terrible classroom student at Birzeit, but I nevertheless learned tons about Palestine. My education arose through all-night tea and hookah sessions with my Palestinian friends, the *adhan* reminding us finally to get some sleep.

On one of these nights I and a fellow student found ourselves about two miles from Birzeit with no transportation. (Even *service* drivers take a few hours to sleep.) Although we were invited to sleep in the home of our friend, it was a lovely evening, so we opted to walk. Just after leaving the small cluster of homes, dogs began howling in the nearby hills. A few soon came into sight, their growls a greater threat than any we had yet faced from occupation soldiers. We climbed a rugged slope and trekked across loose dirt and stones on the ridge alongside the roadway. When headlights approached, we jumped down and hitched a ride home.

The soil of Palestine was lodged beneath my fingernails for over a week. It's one of the few moments of my life that the Holy Land was rendered tactile and knowable.

Feral wildlife has a long history in the region. Lions, crocodiles, cheetahs, elephants, rhinos, giraffes, and water buffaloes once existed in Palestine, evoking its African origin and orientation. We cannot attribute their disappearance to Zionist colonization. Yet we can attribute to Zionists the revival of at least one famed species, the camel.

Camels have been, and continue to be, crucial to the commerce of Africa, the Middle East, and Central Asia, but among Arab and Muslim Americans they tend to induce groans—not from any particular dislike of the animals themselves, but because of their uses in variegated Orientalist imagery. The camel is the great signifier of Arab culture in the West. Whenever a film wishes to denote or connote the Middle East, we hear canned oud music and see sandy dunes traversed peacefully by a caravan of slow-moving camels, usually in silhouette with a blazing sun in the background.

Zionism reproduces this imagery for the sake of ethnic verisimilitude. When I was at Virginia Tech, a Hillel event celebrating

Israel included a camel. (Don't ask me how it managed to get a camel to Blacksburg.) In the touristy areas of Israel, one can take pictures of an authentic Bedouin and his humped conveyance. (To be fair, this is also true of Arab countries.)

Zionists play Arab to inscribe themselves as Indigenous to a foreign geography. Beyond their fondness for camels, they revived a version of Hebrew meant to sound akin to Arabic, claim as Israeli numerous dishes that existed well before 1948, and attempt architectural authenticity by erecting structures in the style of the actual buildings they destroy. It's a reinvention of a landscape that was mythologized by the West in the first place. Israel has destroyed Palestine's natural history physically *and* symbolically.

I am no botanist or biologist, so I am more comfortable discussing people than plants or wildlife. While biologists work with the human animal, I am too engrained in humanist traditions to rely on biology to make sense of culture or politics. Zionists, after all, created a nation-state based on the incongruities of biological determinism.

As to the people of the land, the Palestinians, they only figure into Zionist mythology as relics of the past, fit for display in shows of quaint nostalgia, never as agents fit for self-determination.

꙳

My father-in-law was born in Beit Jala, adjacent to Bethlehem, and spent his first twenty years there before immigrating to the United States as a student. Nobody would rightly call him a quiet man. He is boisterous and gregarious, a wonderful person who sometimes relishes playing the role of trickster. Yet despite his conviviality, he doesn't speak often of his days in Palestine.

I take credit for his emergence as a storyteller. My wife Diana once wondered, "How do you get him to talk so openly about his childhood?"

"It's simple," I replied. "I ask him about it."

I'm damn glad I ask, too. His anecdotes are terrific. Even in the hands of a lesser storyteller, his tales would be interesting simply because of their content.

I love listening to him reflect on life in a West Bank devoid of Jewish settlement. Once enough stories are accumulated, it becomes clear that my father-in-law adores and embodies the natural history of Palestine. His narrative is filled with flora and fauna: olives, figs, pistachios, pomegranates; birds, gazelles, and reptiles; streams, wells, and aquifers; grape leaves, lavish trellises, and homemade wine.

Zaatar once grew wild throughout the hills surrounding Beit Jala.[8] Children hunted birds with old British shotguns. They could explore the surroundings for miles. Such activities exist no longer. Israel controls nearly all of the harvest. Palestinian children with shotguns—or with stones or with even nothing at all—are targets of occupation soldiers. And there's no area of the West Bank wild enough for children to explore unfettered; sooner or later they will run into a checkpoint or a settlement.

The same problems affect the Gaza Strip, on a broader but more microcosmic scale. It is likewise true of the Palestinian citizens of Israel and those who inhabit refugee camps throughout the region. The Palestinian landscape is dominated by the structures of division.

Yet animals remain. Olive trees still age for centuries. The Palestinian people are even more attached to their ancestral land. Perhaps *this* is the natural history of Palestine: the unbelievable endurance of its flora and fauna despite so many threats of eradication; and the persistence of its Indigenes despite the captivity of occupied space.

---

8. Zaatar is a Levantine herb usually mixed with salt, sesame seeds, sumac, and other ingredients to form a popular accessory to bread and olive oil. As with much Eastern Mediterranean foodstuff, Zionists pretend that somehow it is Israeli, though it predates 1948 by many centuries. Then again, some Zionists claim that oranges and cell phones were invented in Israel.

To the great distress of Zionist leaders who have long antici-
pated their demise, the Palestinian people, like the many landscapes
they inhabit, have displayed an extraordinary talent for reinvention,
which in this industrialized world is a necessary precondition of
survival.

THREE

Entry Not Approved

W as I actually hired? According to contract law and hiring protocol, yes. UIUC and its supporters claim that I wasn't technically yet an employee because my appointment was contingent on the approval of the board of trustees, but various factors render that claim insufficient.

First of all, university chancellor Phyllis Wise, system president Robert Easter, and the board of trustees ignored their own statutes, which stipulate that in the event of a hiring issue the dean and department chair convene and consider that issue in conjunction with upper administration. Wise, Easter, and the board acted arbitrarily, without input from relevant faculty bodies.

There's also this statute: "It is the policy of the University to maintain and encourage full freedom within the law of inquiry, discourse, teaching, research, and publication and to protect any member of the academic staff against influences, from within or without the University, which would restrict the member's exercise of these freedoms in the member's area of scholarly interest." Administration is charged with protecting faculty from outside influence. We have considerable evidence that UIUC acted in response to donor pressure.

Again, was I actually an employee? I was according to an authority no less credible than the university itself. On July 22, 2014, just ten days before my firing, UIUC spokeswoman Robin Kaler responded to criticism of my tweets by noting, "Faculty have a wide range of scholarly and political views, and we recognize the freedom-of-speech rights of all of our employees." *Faculty. Employee.* Not a whit of ambiguity here. Wise used the same line in an email to a disgruntled interlocutor on the same day.[9] Provost Ilesanmi Adesida emphatically proclaimed, "He [Salaita] accepted the offer; this had been done since September last year. It is done!"

I had been assigned courses and an office. I had ordered books and a computer. The university had arranged for movers to arrive. Wise herself had invited me to a new faculty reception. My contract began on August 16; board approval wasn't to occur until September 11. My original contract had set a starting date of January 1, 2014, but I pushed it back to summer so I could complete the year at Virginia Tech, where I was a tenured associate professor of English. UIUC induced me to resign that position and, along with it, the protections of tenure. Had I started in January, I might have worked more than nine months before receiving board approval. In the past few decades, the board has approved thousands of hires. Mine is the only one to be rejected.

You don't have to rely on my word to understand that board approval of faculty hires is pro forma. Interim dean Brian Ross, of the College of Letters and Sciences, sent me a letter welcoming me to the faculty. It reads in part: "I am delighted you chose to accept the offered position with our American Indian Studies Program." My contract states: "New academic staff members will receive a formal Notification of Appointment from the Board once the hiring unit has received

---

9. Wrote Wise: "Dear [Redacted]: Thank you for reaching out to us. As you know, our faculty have a wide range of scholarly and political views, and we recognize the freedom of speech rights of all of our employees."

back from the candidate all required documents, so the appointment can be processed." *Will* receive a formal Notification of Appointment. So the appointment *can be* processed. Only those with ideological ties to Israel consider UIUC's actions anything other than a termination of tenured employment. (See Appendix Two for hiring documents.)

The university's Committee on Academic Freedom and Tenure (CAFT), composed of a cross-section of tenured faculty, released a report on December 23, 2014, noting, "As best this committee has been able to determine, the Board has never rejected an appointment that had been generated and reviewed through formal academic channels, and thus administrators and the faculty generally expect that offers of employment for tenured and tenure-track positions will be honored, notwithstanding the standard language included in all letters that they are subject to the Board's approval." Board approval of hires below the level of dean occurs with basic information: name, degree, department, and rank. Board members do not vet pedagogy or scholarship.

The Association of University Professors (AAUP), which developed the regulations for academic freedom in the United States, released a blistering report on UIUC in April 2015. It declares, "The AAUP has taken the view from the beginning that Professor Salaita had already been appointed when he was informed of the chancellor's decision not to forward his appointment to the board of trustees for approval," later concluding that "this investigation has confirmed the Association's position that aborting an appointment in this manner without having demonstrated cause is tantamount to summary dismissal, an action categorically inimical to academic due process." The report illustrates how UIUC tolerated homophobic and white supremacist faculty and reveals that university lawyers attempted to suppress the AAUP investigation.

Another relevant question concerns the prudent use of social media. Folks outside of academe have wondered why it's okay for them to face employer recrimination for mouthing off on Twitter, but somehow it's wrong when it happened to me (or to other scholars). In my case, it's first and foremost a legal matter: UIUC is a public institution; it thus has no standing to fire an employee for political speech. It certainly has no standing to do so based on the desire of wealthy donors. Morally, the question has interesting connotations. One's reaction to or interpretation of my tweets will largely follow her politics. To make it less personal, I present two questions:

- Was my speech on Twitter reason enough to undermine a long tradition of academic freedom (however spotty its application), without which American universities cannot operate?
- Instead of addressing a form of unfairness by making more people subject to limitations on political speech, wouldn't it be more useful to fight for better protection against recrimination for all workers?

The fact that my tweets are open to such distinctive interpretation means they're perfectly appropriate for consideration on college campuses.

"Entry Not Approved" references the paperwork from a September 11, 2014, University of Illinois Board of Trustees meeting in which eight of the nine trustees rejected my appointment as associate professor of American Indian Studies.[10] Here is the entry:

10. The lone dissenter was James Montgomery, an African American civil rights attorney.

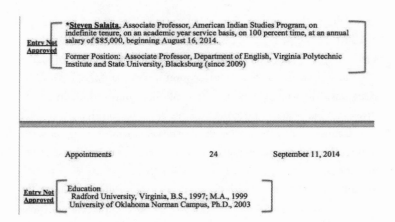

During the vote, the trustees referred to me as "Item 14, page 23, number 4." It's not exactly a prison tattoo, but it nevertheless does an excellent job illuminating the dehumanizing, technocratic conventions of the corporate boardroom. When it comes to budgetary and ideological concerns, we are not human beings, but agenda items.

Such is the tenor of "entry not approved," a technical dictum replete with human interest but wholly oblivious to any iteration of humanity. The university meant it as a public record, but I read it as a thoroughly personal episode, one connected to a much grander and more private vision of universities and the worldly conflicts they embody. An entry submitted as a random professorial appointment was not approved. This bureaucratic flourish forestalls emotion by deploying pragmatic judgment in a passive voice. Nobody, according to the record, is actually responsible for that judgment. Like all acts of bureaucratic management, it was done by fiat of habituation.

I was thus barred from the university. In barring me, the trustees also banished a set of ideas it considers threatening while codifying others it finds appealing (based on administrative interests). The body of the dissident scholar personifies a breach of institutional virtue; he is thus banished from entry as both physical object and intellectual subject. The act of approval or disapproval occurs from spaces beyond the campus. Trustees affixed a gaze to a site of learning indivisible from their own economic geographies. Like most struggles, this one is assiduously symbolic. The symbolism of my firing can be located in important sites of material politics.

There is likely no rationale to this event occurring on September 11, but it entails plenty of symbolism. Palestine is (falsely) implicated in the tragedy. For Palestinians, "entry not approved" pertains to their ancestral land. A Palestinian is likely to hear the command at a checkpoint or in response to a request for a travel permit. "Entry not approved" also pertained at one point to Jewish college and country club applications in the United States. The line is painfully reminiscent of "whites only" signs in southern diners, the exclusivity of an aristocratic soiree, or an electrified fence encircling government secrets. It speaks to so many communities and individuals who experience disapproval through the locutions of an unexamined rectitude.

Islam and Arabs are also implicated in 9/11. As are all individuals who can be made to identify with either. My affiliations are not voluntary. That privilege belongs to those who please and embrace the majority. The 9/11 attacks didn't initiate anything that hadn't already begun, but they accelerated the relegation of moral critique into tidy categories of good and evil, right and wrong, safe and scary, civil and uncivil. If terrorism arises from dogma, then we cannot accept the exercise of top-down power in good faith. All political violence originates in the tenacity of common sense.

FOUR

Uncivil Rites

L ying to children is not merely convenient; it is often ethical.
I don't just passively lie to my young son, who, as of this
writing, is a spry, boisterous two and a half. He deserves better, and
I have higher parenting aspirations. I lie with purpose, aware of the
importance of crafting narratives that supplement the reality I want
him to inhabit, rather than the one in which we actually exist. All
parents—including those who recoil at the exhaustive "all"—teach
our offspring the power of artful rhetoric. A lie is often more tolerable than dishonesty. Lying isn't always dishonest, but dishonesty is
always the stuff from which propaganda is made.

We protect our children from bad things for hundreds of reasons,
but one of them, primal and irrational, is the hope that ignorance can
sustain verisimilitude. We know it cannot. We do it anyway.

I remember vividly the first time I held my son. I had removed
my shirt so he could absorb my warmth. The nurses called it "skin-
to-skin contact," a bonding ritual supposedly rife with psychological and physical benefits. He smelled of lambswool and impending
rain. His fingers flitted, his lips suckling an imaginary nipple. Long
and lean, he had eaten heartily (a habit he still exhibits) and would
soon quietly fall asleep (something that never became habitual).

He arrived with a thick, black mane and a flat, wide nose. His melanin presented itself. He had none of the pastiness common to newborns. My wife, Diana, had wanted a brown child with curly hair; her wish was fulfilled. I cupped my hand to the back of his skull and pulled him to my chest. He gurgled but didn't cry. I rubbed my cheek along the top of his head, damp hair clinging to my stubble. His mother, who had just endured many hours of natural labor, extended her arms. I laid him on her chest and covered them with a blanket. Together they slept.

"I'll do well for this child," I told myself.

Diana returned to work after six weeks, cursing the fact that we don't live in Sweden, and I assumed full-time parental duties. I treasure those days. I learned how to heat milk to a comfortable temperature and undertook the daunting task of keeping an insatiable infant satisfied between breaks when Diana would rush home to breastfeed. As our son grew, we passed the days with long walks, me struggling (and ultimately failing) to find ways to adequately shade him from the sun. (The little guy was fond of pulling down the blanket I draped over the stroller.) I cooked simple meals with him in the crook of my left arm while I stirred pasta or sautéed vegetables with my right. I held him on my stomach as I reclined and read long-neglected novels. I wheeled him into the bathroom whenever I showered. There were no solitary moments. His life was completely integrated into mine—perhaps it might be more accurate to say that my life was completely integrated into his.

As he matured, his future took shape. I could imagine what he would look and be like as an adult—the facial expressions, physical characteristics, dining habits, sense of humor, modes of protestation, personality quirks.

During his six-month checkup, he sat on my lap as the pediatrician monitored his breathing. I noticed fuzzy sideburns and tiny black hairs on his back.

"Doc, give it to me straight," I said. "This boy's gonna look like Sasquatch when he hits puberty, isn't he?"

The doctor, a humorless man, considered my question. "Yes," he finally responded before continuing the examination.

Most children are difficult to classify; their development never coheres to the simplistic categories promoted in parenting books, which are generally useless. ("You don't need that nonsense," a close friend, the majestic Coptic poet Matthew Shenoda, told me while Diana was pregnant. "Just lots of love and some Third World common sense.")

Children achieve wonderful benchmarks: solid food, teething, object permanence, muscle memory. But I was always trained on the emergence of my son's disposition, especially his sense of empathy. It became clear he possessed this attribute when he began talking. "Okay?" he would ask whenever something seemed amiss. His older cousins, my nephews, would roughhouse with me and he would protest in operatic fear.

"Okay, Papa?" he asked whenever I freed myself from the relentless assault of the two rapscallions. I reassured him with a kiss to the cheek and demonstrations of my continued functionality.

When Diana was packing for a weeklong conference, she finally succumbed to tears at the prospect of being away from the little fellow for so long. He put down his dump truck and sauntered to her, burying his face in her neck. "Okay, Mama?" He had recently turned two. It was the biggest indication yet that he would grow into the type of person I so badly want him to become.

On the afternoon of August 2, we enjoyed a typical Saturday: the Blacksburg farmer's market and Bollo's in the morning, followed by a group nap and family time on the back deck. Diana and I lounged in pastel Adirondack chairs while he collected pine cones and deposited them into a charcoal grill. I went inside to sip water and check my email. At that point, I opened my Virginia Tech account only a few times a week. I had already resigned from the institution as a tenured associate professor of English. The account, attached to an address that was my only publicly known information, received little more than hate mail.

That afternoon there was a message from UIUC chancellor Phyllis Wise with the cryptic subject line, "please see attached letter." The body of the message was also vague:

Dear Dr. Salaita,

Please read the attached letter.

Sincerely,

Phyllis M. Wise
Chancellor, University of Illinois at Urbana-Champaign
Swanlund Administration Building
601 East John Street
Champaign, IL 61820
Phone: (217) 333-6290
Fax: (217) 244-4121

Why in the world, I wondered, would the chancellor write me a letter? With a feeling of dread, I opened the attachment to find what appeared to be a termination letter. (See Appendix Two.)

The letter, in true administrative style, was unambiguously ambivalent. Had I been fired? Was I going to be fired? I felt pretty sure I'd been fired, but unsure of the veracity of that feeling.

"Diana! Come inside, please!"

A moment later she peeked into the living room, exhibiting a distinct sort of dishevelment that arises from ensuring a toddler doesn't ingest lighter fluid or deer pellets.

"You have to read this."

"Just tell me what it is."

"No, you have to read it. Seriously."

Skeptical, she walked behind the couch and scanned the screen. I could feel her tension increase along with her recognition.

"Have I been fired?"

"Yes." She was unequivocal.

"What the fuck?" I covered my face with both hands. I was immediately inflicted by a feeling of shame.

He had been dumping picture books from a built-in cabinet. Noticing my anguish, he ambled across the room, stopping next to my left knee. Placing his hand on my thigh, his inky pupils wide with concern, he asked, "Okay, Papa?"

"Yes, my love," I replied, squeezing his hand. "Papa's okay."

FIVE

Survival of the Fitness

It has become popular to call me uncivil. Or intemperate. Or inappropriate. Or angry. Or aggressive. Or any other high-minded adjective that aligns its user with profound state violence while pretending to offer some corrective to a terribly violent world.

I realize it's unseemly to describe myself, but because "unseemly" is an improvement over what many people now call me—eh, why not?

I am a devoted husband and a loving father. I never talk out of turn. I deliberate for long periods before making significant decisions. As is normal for somebody born and raised in Southern Appalachia, I call everybody "sir" or "ma'am." I do not raise my voice at people. I am, in fact, deeply shy and chronically deferential. That is to say, I am civil to a fault.

This exegesis on my disposition probably seems unnecessary, but it's important to distinguish between somebody's persona and his personhood, though in most cases one informs the other. I am uninterested in conducting a debate about the goodness and badness of public figures, a metric whose tabloid overtones displace focus from more pressing issues.

This is the extent of my feelings on the matter: it is precisely because I am a loving person that I so adamantly deplore Israel's behavior.

My discourse might appear uncivil, but such a judgment can never be proffered in an ideological or rhetorical vacuum. Civility and incivility make sense only in frameworks influenced by countless social and cultural valuations, often assisted by misreading or distortion. These terms don't neutrally describe an actor or action. People often deploy the terms to disparage or exalt without having to explain.

Insofar as "civil" is profoundly racialized and has a long history of demanding conformity to the ethos of imperialism and colonization, I frequently choose incivility as a form of communication. (Or it is chosen for me.) This choice is both moral and rhetorical. Anybody familiar with age-old colonial discourses about the suitability of natives for self-governance understands that the language of civilization is profoundly compromised.

Those who decry my "incivility," then, implicate the cultures and histories from which my rhetoric and morality emerge. The accusation is not only disingenuous, but oblique, reliant on allusion and passive-aggressiveness to convey insidious arguments for which its users refuse to accept responsibility.

Colonial taskmasters have perfected the art of disparaging principled critique by summoning moralism. The piety and sanctimony are most evident in hand-wringing about my use of curse words.

While I am proud to share something in common with Richard Pryor, J. D. Salinger, George Carlin, S. E. Hinton, Maya Angelou, Judy Blume, and countless others who have offended the priggish, I confess to being rather confused as to why obscenity is such an issue to those who supposedly devote their lives to analyzing the endless nuances of public expression. Academics are usually eager to contest censorship and deconstruct vague and evangelical charges of vulgarity.

When it comes to defending Israel, though, anything goes. If there's no serious moral or political argument in response to criticism of Israel, then condemn the speaker for various failures of "tone" and "appropriateness." Emphasis now exists on the speaker and not on Israel. A word becomes more relevant than an array of war crimes.

Zionists regularly deploy this strategy to the detriment of phenomena they claim to consider sacrosanct: academic freedom, democracy, integration, inclusiveness, multiculturalism, open debate, free inquiry, dialogue, social justice.

It's tempting to dismiss the strategy as hypocrisy, but other factors exist. We have to consider, first of all, the limits of academic freedom and multiculturalism when they so easily circumscribe opinion and validate Zionist narratives as virtuous. It is also important to assess how Zionists have appointed themselves guardians of discursive and pedagogical respectability, particularly vis-à-vis people of color. Finally, Zionist interests directly oppose communities in academe that wish to effect structural change. It is crucial, then, that we treat Zionists not as a hermetic political bloc, but as an embodiment and custodian of the corporate academy itself.

Even by the tendentious standards of "civility," a term of which anybody should be suspicious because of its colonial sensibilities, my comments on Twitter (and elsewhere) are more defensible than the accusations used to defame me. The most deplorable acts of violence germinate in the spaces of high society. Many genocides have been glorified (or planned) around dinner tables adorned with forks and knives made from actual silver, without a single inappropriate speech act having occurred.

In colonial landscapes, civility is inherently violent. You simply have to learn to discuss violence the right way.

Deploying language that undermines the commonplaces of respectable speech threatens the authority of the elite, who have the power to name as "civil" and "uncivil" those elements of our rhetoric that impose meaning (or cliché) on the various struggles of the world.

In most conversations about my termination, Israel's war crimes go unmentioned, yet it is impossible to understand my tweets without that necessary context. My strong language—and I should point out that much of my language is also gentle—arises in response to demonstrable acts of brutality that in a better world would raise widespread rancor.

You tell me which is worse: cussing in condemnation of the murder of children or using impeccable manners to justify their murder. I no more want to be "respectable" according to the epistemologies of colonial wisdom than I want to kill innocent people with my own hands. Both are articulations of the same moral rot.

In eleven years as a faculty member, I have fielded exactly zero complaints about my pedagogy. Every peer evaluation of my instruction—the gold standard for judging teaching effectiveness—has been stellar. Student evaluations ranked higher than the mean every time I collected them. I was an incredibly popular teacher.

Yet people affiliated with the University of Illinois have impugned my ability to teach. Criticism of my pedagogy uniformly arises without evidence, the primary basis on which scholarship is judged. One thus wonders what type of standards my critics uphold in the classroom.

Students are capable of serious discussion, of formulating responses, of thinking through discomfort, of rearranging convention, of unlearning the commonplaces of discourse governed by corporate desire. They like my teaching because I refuse to infantilize them; I treat them as thinking adults, instead. I have never disrespected a student under my charge. I have never told a student what to think.

Nor have I ever shut down an opinion. I encourage students to argue with me. They take me up on the offer. I sometimes change my viewpoints in return. My philosophy is simple: teach them the modes and practices of critical thought and let them figure out things on their own.

The hand-wringing about students is pious, precious claptrap, a pretext that exploits an amorphous demographic to clean the stench from a rotten argument raised to validate an unjustifiable decision. I won't impugn the classroom abilities of those who have proved themselves dishonest because I have no evidence to suggest they are bad teachers, only bad thinkers. I certainly wish they would have adhered to the same professional standard when commenting on my teaching ability.

Troublesome assumptions underlie questions about my fitness for the classroom. It is impossible to separate questions about my "civility" from broader narratives of inherent Arab violence. This sort of accusation has been used to discredit people of color (and other minorities) in academe for many decades. Administrators and the public monitor and scrutinize our actions in a manner to which our white colleagues are rarely subject. It is crucial to train us in the ways of civility lest our emotions dislodge the ethos our superiors hold so dear.

For this reason, the 2013 American Studies Association resolution to boycott Israeli academic institutions led to anxiety about the changing demographics of the field. Respectable academics have learned well from Israel.

Many white academics feel empowered to decide on behalf of the colonized how they should speak and what they should say when they are afforded the opportunity. The impulse arises from their default power, which they needn't recognize in order to enact. Nor do they need to acknowledge that power to reinforce the structures that sustain it. There's a reason they get so indignant when anybody points it out to them.

Such professors like to think they uphold the decency of the profession. In reality, they merely fortify the authority in which they're so comfortably ensconced. ·

When it comes to opposing colonization, there is no need for dissimulation, which is the preferred vocabulary of the cocktail party and committee meeting. I could make a case that dissimulation is immoral. It is undoubtedly boring.

When I say something, I have no desire to conceal meaning in oblique and wishy-washy diction. This is especially so when I respond to the various horrors of state violence and the depravity of those who justify it. On campus, such forthrightness is unconventional. But no tenet of academic freedom considers failure to adhere to convention a fireable offense.

Professors are often punished for disrupting convention in informal ways, however. My case is interesting because administrators ignored the de facto standards that regulate our behavior and exercised their power directly. This portends poorly for any scholar who isn't a sycophant.

I prefer not to lose sight of the point that what I say is eminently more ethical than what hordes of well-heeled Zionist operatives suggest without having the conviction to actually state. In attacking me, they implicitly (and sometimes explicitly) condone brutal violence and imply that passionate condemnation of injustice is somehow worse than injustice itself. I have a large body of scholarship and public writing. I have a teaching record. It is incumbent on those who debase me to consult them.

There are so many myths to debunk, but ultimately it comes down to this: people with doctorates who make claims unsupported by evidence and who uncritically repeat terms like "incivility" as if it describes anything other than their own dull prejudice are the ones most unfit to teach college.

SIX

Imaginary Students

I'm often asked if I regret writing the tweets that supposedly got me fired.

I understand why folks ask the question, though their motivations differ. Sometimes it's a gambit intended to provoke admission of wrongdoing. At other times it's a sincerely curious query. I'm a humanities academic, though, trained to seek complexity even in the most exquisite forms of simplicity. Few binaristic questions are as easy to answer as they are to ask, especially when they possess conspicuous and complicated subtexts. I can't simply say no or yes because it's important to read questions in context of what they suggest, not merely what they desire. In this case, there's too much of a reliance on linear induction. Would I have written the tweets knowing I would get fired? Of course not. But this is a much different inquiry than asking if I regret publishing the controversial tweets.

Would anybody swim in the ocean if that person knew she would be mauled by a bull shark? It's always a possibility when we dive into the surf, and yet beaches see no shortage of bathers. We make decisions based on conscious or unconscious assessment of risk. Hypotheticals inform decisions, but moral signification exists most pertinently at the moment of deciding. I tweeted without any meaningful sense that I would be targeted by political opponents who might misread meaning and then undermine my livelihood. Nor do I believe that my tweets warrant such punishment even absent the protection of free speech.

Answering the question is particularly difficult in corporate media, whose formats reward zippy sound bites and pithy banter, two areas in which I have little skill. (Forgive my boastfulness.) Sometimes it takes me about ten seconds just to get started, which can constitute the entire time frame a host will allow a guest to respond. I am a reliable purveyor of dead air. I don't simply find these formats personally unlikeable. They contribute to a political culture replete with platitudes and patriotic sloganeering.

A major complication of the question is that I don't believe the tweets are the only reason for my termination. They're metonymical, surely, and perhaps partly responsible, but not in ways I would call definitive. Fanatical Zionists can always find a pretext for being punitive, but their punitive strategies occupy broader questions. (Please note: I am not calling all Zionists fanatical, but identifying as fanatical those who seek to punish their ideological opponents.) Here are some of the factors that contributed to my firing:

- My vocal support of Boycott, Divestment, and Sanctions (BDS).
- My ethnic identity. (It is more nuanced than simply "Palestinian.")
- The profoundly corrupt politics of Illinois.
- Having had the misfortune of being hired at a campus home to former AAUP president Cary Nelson.
- Israel's failed propaganda efforts during 2014's Operation Protective Edge.
- The interference of wealthy donors.
- The corporatization of American universities.

- The increased authority governing boards have conferred to themselves.
- The delegation of labor on campus into deeply stratified economic classes.
- The weak and impressionable leadership of Phyllis Wise.

What happened to me has been happening to ethnic, sexual, and cultural minorities in academe for decades, African Americans especially, and it continues to happen today. A shameful irony is that Jews were long marginalized in the academy because of their supposed dangers to Anglo civility, victim to rationalizations for their exclusion that, sadly, don't look terribly different than the ones now being used against supporters of Palestinian human rights.

I thus want to honor those before and alongside me and those in the future on whose behalf we struggle for a better world. Any cursory review of the history of American universities shows that academic freedom isn't universally accessible. The suppression of Blackness and Indigeneity predates the purge of Palestine and in many ways contextualizes and sustains it.

An outstanding case is that of Angela Davis, who was fired (twice) and falsely indicted for murder. A new assistant professor of philosophy at UCLA in 1969, Davis earned the ire of then-Governor Ronald Reagan, who orchestrated the termination of her employment because of her membership in the Communist Party. Her revolutionary politics around race and gender, along with her Black Panther affiliation, also enacted the UC Regents' anxiety. Davis won a lawsuit for her reinstatement, but in 1970 the regents fired her for "inflammatory language," a cruder version of the civility rationale. The only thing Davis's language inflamed was the interests of the white male elite. She went on to a luminous career as a scholar and prison abolition activist, but that career has never escaped sensitivity to inflammation. It shouldn't pass our notice that the main issue inspiring condemnation of Davis these days is her support of BDS.

The regulation of deviant bodies, ideas, and identities has influenced American campuses since their inception. With some exceptions, the ethos of the university as a site of special intellectual dispensation came into existence based on exclusion. My situation makes no sense outside of this context. Nothing in academe makes sense at the level of individuality. We are in it together, whether or not we want to be.

As to the reasons for my termination, BDS and Operation Protective Edge are central.

Let's start with BDS, a nonviolent form of resistance to Israeli colonization, initiated by a call from Palestinian civil society in 2005. "Civil society" refers to civic, political, and educational organizations. In recent years, BDS has become a crucial element of organizing around Palestine. A number of powerful institutions have endorsed BDS in recent years, including trade unions, scholarly associations, and university senates.

Academic boycott, one facet of BDS, has lately generated great results, as numerous scholarly associations have pledged to adhere to the call from Palestinian civil society, most notably the American Studies Association (ASA), whose 2013 boycott resolution inspired widespread debate. (The ASA was not, in fact, the first US-based scholarly group to pass a boycott resolution; that superlative belongs to the Association for Asian American Studies [AAAS], which did it in March 2013.)

I have been a vocal proponent of BDS and academic boycott for many years and wrote a number of high-profile pieces supporting the ASA resolution. Contrary to popular perception, academic boycott does not target individuals, only institutions. This is not to say that academic boycott does not affect individuals; in some cases it does. Like all movements with a material aim—in this case to end the occupation of Palestine—it necessarily alters both interpersonal relationships and individual rites of affiliation. It does so only through the standard that to be subject to boycott an individual must act as a representative of the Israeli government (including as an emissary of one of the state's universities—this precludes normal public statements of affiliation). The limits on personal autonomy, then, remain fully in the individual's control.

BDS has the attention of major pro-Israel organizations and the Israeli government, which has devoted considerable resources to opposing it. Binyamin Netanyahu discusses it frequently, always with visible disgust. It has inspired legislation in New York, Maryland, and Illinois (subsequently defeated) to defund institutions and departments with ASA membership. (Illinois went on to pass an amended bill, SB1761, by unanimous vote in May 2015.) A significant portion of a 2014 conference organized by AIPAC (American Israel Public Affairs Committee) explored strategies to contain BDS. It is a hot topic among pro-Israel organizations. (Quick aside: as a grassroots movement with no formal leadership and no external funding sources, BDS is impossible to contain.)

As to Operation Protective Edge, it resulted in largely terrible press for Israel. The viciousness of the assault was beamed around the world, which led to intensive criticism of the Israeli government. Images of dead infants and toddlers flooded social media. Even mainstream news outlets that normally sanitize Israeli violence covered the invasion from more critical points of view. In fewer than two months, Israel killed more than 2,100 Palestinians, 551 of them children; displaced 475,000 Palestinians in Gaza; destroyed 18,000 homes; damaged 244 schools; and repeatedly bombed hospitals and UN shelters. The inhabitants of Gaza suffered severe food and water shortages and had to subsist without electricity. According to a Ynetnews.com poll, 95 percent of Israelis supported this barbarity. Only 3 to 4 percent described Israel's actions as excessive. We're not talking about being opposed to the operation—just those who considered the firepower excessive. In fact, 45 percent of Israelis described the level of fire-power as *insufficient*. A *Jerusalem Post* survey found that 86.5 per-cent of Israelis opposed a ceasefire. The campaign isolated Israel more than ever before.

In the span of one month in 2014, I was terminated from a tenured position. Megan Marzec, the student council president at Ohio University (OU), was serially harassed for condemning Is-rael by pouring a fake bucket of blood on her head as a spoof of the "ice bucket challenge"; upper administrators at OU participated in the condemnation, though their only legitimate responsibility was to affirm the speech rights of their student rather than entertain-ing baseless accusations from professional trolls. Bruce Shipman, an Episcopal chaplain at Yale, was fired for "anti-Semitic remarks" that in no way endorsed anti-Semitism.[11] Brant Rosen, a rabbi critical of Israeli policies, resigned under pressure from his con-gregation for daring to condemn Operation Protective Edge. That September, the AMCHA Initiative, which is essentially devoted to getting professors fired, released a list of 218 scholars it deemed inadequately Zionist. Not long after, a cohort of anonymous cow-ards launched the Canary Mission, an online database to moni-tor student activists, intended to subvert their future employment prospects. Palestine Legal, a group protecting the civil and human rights of Israel's critics, has recorded hundreds of complaints of harassment by pro-Israel outfits in the past few years.

BDS and Operation Protective Edge deeply inform these phe-nomena. While it has long been a staple of Zionist organizing to exert pressure on institutions to discipline and punish the recal-citrant, there's something distinctly grievous at play here. I don't know that, empirically speaking, there's been an uptick of instances

---

11. In a letter to the *New York Times*, Shipman wrote, "Deborah E. Lipstadt makes far too little of the relationship between Israel's policies in the West Bank and Gaza and growing anti-Semitism in Europe and beyond."

of Zionist repression in the past year, but it *feels* like there has; it's worth considering what gives rise to that feeling.

Israel is losing the PR battle, the proverbial hearts and minds. Its supporters, in turn, are lashing out with the sort of desperation endemic to any strong party in decline. They are punitive and belligerent in the absence of honest debate. This is about undemocratic power reasserting itself, refusing to cede a word to Palestinians in a severely compromised public discourse. It is, simply stated, colonial paranoia.

This psychology should be easy for anybody to see. If your first impulse upon encountering a viewpoint you dislike is to punish the speaker, then you tacitly confess that your position has no merit (or that you don't quite have a position so much as a superstition). Anybody not stuck in the dogmas of ethnocracy would consider reexamining that position. Zionism, of course, is not merely stuck in the dogmas of ethnocracy; many of its traditions embody them.

And now civility is spreading through universities as quickly as settlers overwhelmed the North American continent. Rutgers University has a Project Civility. The University of Missouri promotes civility through its "Show Me Respect" program. The University of Tennessee doesn't abide by mere Principles of Community, but by "Principles of Civility and Community." Rice University requires job applicants to sign its Standard of Civility in which an employee "serves as a representative of the University, displaying courtesy, tact, consideration and discretion in all interactions with other members of the Rice community and with the public." One-time free speech doyen Nicolas Dirks, now chancellor of UC-Berkeley, proclaimed in September 2014 that "we can only exercise our right to free speech insofar as we feel safe and respected in doing so, and this in turn requires that people treat each other with civility. Simply put, courteousness and respect in words and deeds are basic preconditions to any meaningful exchange of ideas. In this sense, free speech and civility are two sides of a single coin—the coin of open, democratic society."

Administrators love the word: it means anything they want it to mean and implies something sinister without its user having to justify or explain. The term encapsulates the sheer force of panic that pervades the elite when they need to find an effortless way to hamper debate, which is usually inimical to their interests. No argument to be made? No problem. It's quite easier simply to forestall the debate.

This phenomenon is particularly troublesome when it comes to faculty governance. Do we want experts in their fields in charge of hiring? Or do we cede that difficult task to the Simon Wiesenthal Center?[12]

The term "civility" is critical to the strategic vision of groups like Hillel and the David Project. University of Illinois administrators seem to be following that strategic vision, to the point that they sound like bluntly allegorical characters in a political novel. Let's take a look:

Handbook strategy: "While name-and-shame tactics can be put to positive effect, they can also easily backfire and do more harm than good. We need to learn the art of being disagreeable in the most agreeable possible fashion." —David Bernstein, executive director of the David Project

Actual quote: "[A]ny student of any faith or background must feel confident that personal views can be expressed and that philosophical disagreements with a faculty member can be debated in a civil, thoughtful and mutually respectful manner." —Phyllis Wise, UIUC Chancellor.

Handbook strategy: "ICC's Research and Analysis Operation includes: An early-warning system that identifies the likelihood of

---

12. The Simon Wiesenthal Center intervened in my hiring. Its executive director, Rabbi Meyer H. May, and campus outreach coordinator, Aron Hier, sent a letter to President Easter, saying, "What possible prestige can Salaita add to the UI faculty when in truth, he is a misguided 'academic' who spews such venomous and mendacious analogies?"

anti-Israel activity on campus. [. . .] Tracking of pro-Israel and anti-Israel activity on campus."—Israel on Campus Coalition

Actual quote: "There are scores of [Salaita's] tweets. I have screen captures." —Cary Nelson, faculty fellow, Israel on Campus Coalition.[13]

Handbook strategy: "Hillel welcomes a diversity of student perspectives on Israel and strives to create an inclusive, pluralistic community where students can discuss matters of interest and/or concern about Israel and the Jewish people in a civil manner." —Hillel Israel Guidelines

Actual quote: "As chancellor, it is my responsibility to ensure that all perspectives are welcome and that our discourse, regardless of subject matter or viewpoint, allows new concepts and differing points of view to be discussed in and outside the classroom in a scholarly, civil and productive manner." —Wise

Handbook strategy: "In light of the alarming rise in global anti-Semitism and the unwillingness of university or government officials to protect Jewish students from campus-based anti-Semitic activity, it is fair to say that when Jewish students return to school in the fall, they will be the single-most vulnerable students on campus." —Tammi Rossman-Benjamin, cofounder of AMCHA Initiative; contributor to *The Case Against Academic Boycotts of Israel*, coedited by Cary Nelson

Actual quote: "We [UI trustees] were sort of stunned that anyone [Salaita] would write such blatantly anti-Semitic remarks." —Christopher Kennedy, Chairman of the UI Board of Trustees (Kennedy rotated off the board in January 2015.)

Handbook strategy: "On campuses and other places where anti-Israel groups act in a disruptive manner, write and promulgate civility petitions calling on all parties to engage in a respectful discussion."—Bernstein

---

13. Yes; I, too, find this creepy.

Actual quote: "We must constantly reinforce our expectation of a university community that values civility as much as scholarship." —Kennedy

Actual quote: "What we cannot and will not tolerate at the University of Illinois are personal and disrespectful words or actions that demean and abuse either viewpoints themselves or those who express them." —Wise

Handbook Strategy: "Unfairly choosing a side, under false pretense, is to shut down a productive and meaningful discussion. This can only cause more tensions and conflict. It takes away OUR voice." —UC-Berkeley's Anti-Divestment Talking Points.[14]

Actual quote: "Professor Salaita's approach indicates that he would be incapable of fostering a classroom environment where conflicting opinions could be given equal consideration, regardless of the issue being discussed." —UI president Robert Easter

I'm most saddened not by the organized campaigns that clearly have the ear of upper administrators, but by the fact that university leadership these days is so inane and unimaginative. These traits, when natural, are profitable qualities. When feigned, they are excellent career choices.

The role of BDS in campus suppression is noteworthy. Pro-Israel groups that exert influence on administrators have made it a priority to combat the movement. (The war imagery is theirs, not mine.) In many executive suites, they encounter receptive audiences. Administrative receptiveness isn't necessarily the result of aversion to Palestinian nationalism (though many deans, provosts, and presidents are indeed averse to all things Palestine). Administrators don't like what BDS represents, beyond its Palestine advocacy: grassroots organizing, faculty autonomy, antiracism, decolonization, systemic critique,

---

14. The best thing in the document: "AVOID a debate on the Middle East. Supporters of the bill would like to argue on this platform." I wish I were creative enough to make up this stuff.

class consciousness, democratic cooperation. Zionism is invested in the corporate university, so for administrators the principle of orthodoxy prevails despite whatever nuances of political outlook may exist.

Please bear in mind: Kennedy admitted that in a board meeting a student representative read aloud some of my tweets and then the board decided I was anti-Semitic and that therefore they couldn't have me on campus. A year had passed from the time I submitted my application to the moment I received an offer. The board nullified that year with a perfunctory Google search. It ignored a plethora of university rules regarding the hiring and firing of professors. It abrogated the work and vision of the American Indian Studies Program. And it damaged the university's ability to function normally based on a desire to appease donors. The board accomplished all of this under the guise of multicultural valor—that is, protecting the campus from intolerance and discomfort.

Please also bear in mind that board members have zero qualifications to evaluate teaching or scholarship. They don't teach college. They know nothing about Indigenous peoples, American Indians, the Israel-Palestine conflict, Arab Americans, Palestine, the Middle East, Pacific Islanders, military occupation, Native nationalism, literary criticism, hermeneutics, critical theory, decolonization, scholarship, journal publishing, peer review, university presses, departmental service, advising, grading, curriculum, or how to compose a solitary footnote. How exactly this qualifies them to make hiring decisions on behalf of the American Indian Studies Program is a mystery.

Shortly after the board meeting in which I was formally terminated, Kennedy gave an interview to the local newspaper, the Champaign-Urbana *News-Gazette*. The article notes, "The UI held off commenting because officials didn't want to put out a statement that would make it more difficult to reach a settlement with Salaita, [Kennedy] said. If Salaita couldn't find another job, that might 'make him push harder to come,' he said."

This passage illuminates Kennedy's ignorance of academe.[15] He imagined it possible to get another job between the time I received the letter and the start of my contract: fourteen days. Anyone with rudimentary knowledge of academic hiring knows that it's impossible to get a tenured position in two weeks—less than a month before the start of fall semester, to boot. I wasn't even able to get an adjunct position or a contract course, much less a tenured gig, because departments staff and schedule their classes months in advance. Such managerial ignorance is more common in universities these days. People from the business or political world take charge of governing boards and pretend that campus is a Fortune 500 company, with no regard for the customs and practices of academe. They intervene in matters in which they have no experience, relying on the protocols of the private sector.

Questions arise about funding, but they have an easy answer. Every bureaucratic decision in this era of neoliberal policy is in some way about money. The university doesn't necessarily receive a windfall from those quick to complain about criticism of Israel. Would-be donors who complained about my hire cited figures of a few hundred thousand. This is chump change to any huge research university and illustrates how cheaply upper administrators can be bought. Universities, anyway, don't quantify contributions based on vertical spreadsheets; the overall health of the brand functions as a ubiquitous asset.

The value of the Zionist donors isn't merely about bank balances; it's about respectability and the unquantifiable value that accompanies it. Siding with Israel is ultimately about political ambition, conformity, establishment bona-fides, state power—in

---

15. My favorite Kennedy quote concerns James Kilgore, another UIUC instructor who experienced public controversy. "We want to be respectful of the fact that we operate on taxpayer's [sic] money and tuition ... and people paying tuition who have will have [sic] concerns about underwriting this lifestyle." Funny, nobody seemed too concerned about taxpayer money underwriting the lifestyle of Jerry Sandusky.

other words, maintaining the status quo. It's about keeping power consolidated among the elite. It's about not setting the terrible precedent of allowing the colonized a say in their own futures.

Political capital coheres, in a way that can never be precisely measured, by supporting the preferred position of the elite. There's rarely risk in siding with the powerful, but never is there dignity in such a choice. Academics themselves are often complicit in restrictions on freedom, so I don't think it's helpful to create a firm distinction between faculty and administration. The distinction should be made in light of an individual's affinities. One needn't be an administrator to supplement administrative interests.

We ought to complicate academic freedom even as we vigorously defend it. For example, contingent faculty have no functional academic freedom. Administrators can punish their speech through the tactic of contract nonrenewal. It's not just finances that compel administrators to rely more heavily on untenured labor. It's a mechanism of plutocratic control, ensuring a power balance that strongly favors the administration. The government has long relied on the private workplace to stifle speech rights; whereas one (hypothetically) cannot be imprisoned for speech, one can be fired by private employers for it. It's a further entanglement of state and corporation. And a further entanglement of corporation and university.

Academic freedom is not impervious or unchanging. It must constantly be reinvigorated and reassessed. Structures of inequality influence how academic freedom is perceived and practiced. The rites of campus governance usually skew in the direction of convention. One way this happens is through unexamined commonplaces of language.

Scholarship, for instance, is never supposed to be "political." Yet what does "political" mean in this context? Anything that states an unorthodox commitment. Scholars are supposed to be above such trifling pursuits. We demystify the things we study, but we don't participate in them. We explicate, but we do not manipulate. We are like the film crew of a nature show: we document and explain, but never intervene when one animal devours another. To be called "political" is immediately to become suspect among one's colleagues, to be marked as "radical," another term with its own history of coerciveness. Serious scholars can never be radical.

Let's assess the term most relevant to our current situation: "civility," which, along with the functions I examine above, is a reboot of the longstanding canard of "collegiality." I believe that "civility," although it performs the same coercive rhetoric as "collegiality," is far more insidious and threatening. Before I explain why, though, I want to give a quick overview of how something that sounds so innocuous, even desirable, is in fact repressive.

I've mentioned informal modes of repression. They're not informal in the sense of being random, but of being unauthorized or extralegal. All industrial democracies rely to some degree on informal repression, what Noam Chomsky called "manufacturing consent" and Antonio Gramsci, before him, termed "hegemony."[16] It is endemic to universities in particular because the conceits of shared governance and academic freedom must be delimited without open suppression (though open suppression happens plenty).

Hence collegiality as a measure of performance. It is a sprawling and subjective word, which is precisely its utility.

Valuable ideas disrupt, reorder, undermine, confront, subvert, unsettle, upset, menace, admonish, forebode. Critical thinking is fundamentally incompatible with conformity, which is collegiality's primary desire. Collegiality largely performs two functions: it

---

16. Gramsci conceived of hegemony as the rule of one socioeconomic class over another. The class being ruled proffers consent based on the commonsensical values of the elite, which come to be accepted as universal.

can be used as a pretext to punish somebody whose work is stellar but who doesn't connect with colleagues (here the problems of race, class, gender, sexuality, and culture should be obvious); and it can name unconventional scholarship as inferior because it doesn't recycle established ideas and methodologies.

Collegiality is the etiquette of submission. It's impossible to be collegial when challenging the common sense of corporate dominion, no matter how politely you state the criticism.

Now, collegiality has given way to "civility," which creates a new set of challenges to academic freedom. The usefulness of the term as a silencing mechanism is apparent by how many upper administrators have embraced it. Its function is identical to that of collegiality, but it more explicitly evokes colonial violence. There is a terrible irony in using "uncivil" to describe supporters of Palestine (or any other site of decolonization): the accusation locates the recipient in the wretchedness of sub-humanity, but implicates the speaker in centuries of colonization and genocide.

Don't forget: I was hired in the American Indian Studies Program. I still shake my head that UIUC administrators decided to rationalize their abrogation of academic freedom and faculty governance by invoking the terminology of New World colonization. It puts me in mind of George W. Bush calling his war on Iraq a crusade. It's another reminder that there's no appreciable correlation between intelligence and authority.

By the way, I shake my head, but I'm not surprised. Calling my sort of discourse uncivil isn't just a gaffe; it's a conscious statement of institutional values of neoliberalism, which requires dogged political supervision. Colonization is central to the conditions of neoliberalism, on and off campus.

The university's actions are a deliberate attack on the fields of American Indian and Indigenous Studies, and on ethnic studies and the humanities more broadly. As throughout American history, Natives are an inconvenience to a grander social vision that cannot be realized without violence, and that erases the elements of Indigeneity that it cannot appropriate. An assumption underlying many justifications of the administration's decision is that Indigenous peoples cannot make autonomous choices; they require the oversight of their more sage and responsible superiors. It is a perfect allegory of federal Indian policy, only it's not actually allegorical.

A final word on civility: Even if we reduce the term to the crude, coercive context in which university administrators deploy it—something we should never do—those administrators still end up on the wrong side. Cheerleaders of civility have been vicious throughout this affair, common when pro-Israel groups target scholars and students. Palestinians and their allies face barrages of racist invective and verbal abuse to accompany the more civilized practices of microaggression and character assassination.

The advocates of civility are particularly nasty toward women of color. Christopher Kennedy dismissed Ojibwe scholar Jeani O'Brien in a much-circulated email, suggesting that her only useful contribution would be silence.[17] Anybody who criticizes practices of colonization in Palestine or North America will experience tremendous vitriol, plenty of it from liberal sources. People of color are fully familiar with these sorts of indignities, which do not emerge from the civilized world so much as they define it.

On the other hand, the kindness and generosity of the uncivilized has been stunning. There are hundreds of Arab stereotypes, one of which, in my experience, is entirely true: we express love through food. I've been offered more to eat since my firing than Attila the Hun's army could consume in a year. In fact, folks of all backgrounds have shared unbelievable hospitality. People

---

17. O'Brien began an email, "I will be brief," and sent two short paragraphs. Kennedy's full response: "You were not brief enough."

have offered money, homes, encouragement, acupuncture, yoga via skype, dental care. It's been, in a word, love. Unfiltered, undiluted love.

If this is incivility, then I eagerly accept my confinement to the dignity of the uncivil.

Let's examine another apparently trenchant word, "students." The administration does everything for the students' sakes, right? Never mind that through administrative behavior students have been rigorously patronized and infantilized. Which students are administrators purporting to help?

The students in this instance aren't communities of actual human beings, but an invention of university management; the most privileged among the student body are beneficiaries of the administration's magnanimity. Students of color, queer and transgender students, low-income students, students in the margins—management rarely includes them in its deliberations; they are useful only insofar as the conceits of multiculturalism can foreclose real democratic participation. No matter how much tuition these students pay, no matter how much they contribute to the vibrancy of intellectual life on campus, they can never be students quite as authoritatively as their normative counterparts.

This is a problem of access and representation on many campuses. UIUC is happy to feature American Indian Studies in its diversity pamphleteering, but is much less eager to support even nominal acts of departmental sovereignty.

Students on the margins, in fact, are constantly made to justify their existence in the elegant spaces of academe. Take the oft-repeated contention that Jewish students would be uncomfortable in my classes.

I leave aside the assumption that discomfort is somehow inimical to a useful education and the qualifications of gentiles to decide who is or isn't Jewish. I would never wish on Jewish students even a hint of acrimony, one reason why it is so discomfiting that they are homogenized as proto-Zionists in this characterization of my pedagogy.

I oppose the policies of the state of Israel—that's the extent of my engagement with "Jewish culture," which is to say I have little engagement with it at all. I'm not indifferent to Jews or to Judaism. I simply do not approach the Israel-Palestine conflict as a special feature of Jewish culture, nor do I implicate that culture in the behavior of the Israeli state. I'm uninterested in Christianity and Islam in exactly the same way. Criticism of Israel cannot fundamentally be anti-Semitic unless we concede that the state's existence only affects Jews. Arabs are central to Israel's composition in every possible way. If people feel attacked on a cultural level when somebody condemns a nation-state, then that's a problem of ethnonationalism, not of political critique.[18] There's nothing in my record as a scholar or teacher that indicates even a scintilla of anti-Semitism; it doesn't take long, on the other hand, to find vigorous condemnation of it.

An inversion suffices to make the point: take any of the countless Zionist ideologues running classrooms. It's possible, likely even, that they support, at least tacitly, ethnic cleansing, military occupation, displacement, home demolition, ethnocracy[19]—in short, a profoundly undemocratic state whose violations of human rights are well documented.

How are Palestinian, Arab, or Muslim students to feel in a class run by a Zionist ideologue? We needn't cite overt racists of the

18. Ethnonationalism conjoins feelings of nationalistic ardor with rigid standards of ethnic belonging. West Bank settlers practice a form of ethnonationalism, as do Holland's Party for Freedom, Saudi Arabia's royal family, and the English Defence League. Ethnonationalism doesn't necessarily entail biological determinism (the notion that one's biology ensures inborn characteristics), but it always enacts racialized criteria for its version of national identity. It often accommodates or incorporates homophobia and sexism. American ethnonationalism is no exception: the terms "bitch" and "faggot" so easily condemn those who eschew the demands of compulsory patriotism.

19. Ethnocracy describes a political system in which rights and privileges are reserved to those who belong to a particular ethnic group, as defined by the state.

Likudnik variety to find examples of this phenomenon. Here, for instance, is *Nation* columnist and Brooklyn College professor Eric Alterman in 2002 after Israel dropped a one-ton bomb on Hamas leader Salah Shehade's apartment complex in Gaza, killing several civilians, including eight children:

> I don't know if killing the military chief of Hamas, together with his family, is an effective military measure—as surely someone will rise to replace him and it will make a lot more people angry, perhaps even angry enough to become suicide bombers. It may not bring Israel and the Palestinians any closer to peace or mutual security. But I don't have a moral problem with it.
>
> Hamas is clearly at war with Israel. Hamas feels empowered to strike Israeli civilians inside Israel proper and not just on the war zone of West Bank. Sheik Salah Shehada could have protected his family by keeping away from them. He didn't and owing to his clear legitimacy as a military target, they are dead too.
>
> So tough luck, fella.
>
> War is hell.

Paul Berman, at different points affiliated with UC-Irvine and NYU, has written of "mass pathology" in Palestine and of Muslims "drunk on the idea of slaughter," both problems contributing to "apocalyptic and death-obsessed mass movements." Alan Dershowitz, the erstwhile Felix Frankfurter Professor of Law at Harvard, has provided the following wisdom: "Hamas wants Palestinians civilians, especially babies, to be killed by Israelis rockets. They want Palestinian babies to be killed precisely so that they can display the kind of photographs that were shown around the world: a grieving father holding his dead baby, presumably killed by an Israeli rocket. For years, I have called this Hamas' 'dead baby strategy.'"[20]

Mira Sucharov, a scholar of political science at Carleton University who has singlehandedly preserved the full array of colonial

---

20. Dershowitz isn't the first to deploy the phrase "dead baby strategy," though he takes credit for its invention. As if it's something to be proud of.

platitudes, recently observed:

> The fact of an imbalance of military and material power between
> Israelis and Palestinians helps explain how different are internal
> Palestinian (including Palestinian Diaspora) politics from in-
> ternal Israeli (including Jewish Diaspora) politics. It also helps
> explain why the kind of Palestinian "peace activists" and critical
> journalists and academics we see among some Israelis and some
> Diaspora Jews are less visible. Where are the Palestinian Yos-
> sis (Beilin and Sarid), one might ask? Where is the Palestinian
> Amira Hass or Gideon Levy?

If we expunge the passive-aggressive and self-righteous features of
Sucharov's passage (a monumental undertaking), it's possible to understand what she's really saying: the Palestinians aren't as morally
and intellectually evolved as the Jews. Scare quotes are necessary
around "peace activists" because it's a category Sucharov can define
only by her experience of the term. No matter how loudly Palestinians talk (and practice) peace, their voices are nonexistent unless validated by Diaspora Jews. Palestinians objectively exist most visibly
in the framework of Jewish subjectivity. It is thus the responsibility
of those Jews to oversee and engineer a judicious resolution to the
conflict, one that, as Sucharov makes clear elsewhere, legitimizes the
conquest of 1948 and ensures a permanent Jewish majority. In more
honest moments we call this sort of desire "eugenics."

Palestinian students hear such things all the time inside and
beyond the college classroom. It makes them stronger, yes, but fortitude does little to change the hypocrisies of campus life. The politics
of affect weren't made for our benefit.

I have been maligned for supposed excesses that are common
among Zionist scholars. The main difference is that I've never actually disparaged any group of people, Jews included. Those I cite
cannot make the same argument. What they can do, however, is
access and invigorate centers of power that regenerate colonial logic.

This double standard is not just an oversight or disconnect; it's a structural problem of disparate power based on ethnicity and religion. In my case, an imagined hostility devoid of evidence is enough to summarily fire me, but in the case of the Zionist instructor the support of racial violence is *actually real*. The fact that nobody ever asks about the comfort of the Arab or Muslim student in the first place illuminates the presence of Zionist violence in the mythologies of civility.

It's always the marginal, the undesirable, the wretched, who must justify their humanity to the majority. The latent violence of the normative, meanwhile, gets to define itself as benign.

SEVEN

The Pro-Israel Activist Handbook, Unabridged

Here are some things you won't find in those Zionist guides to campus activism:

- Stick to the facts.
- Invoke the work of leading scholars.
- Reference international law, particularly the Fourth Geneva Convention.
- Human rights groups are excellent sources of information.
- Palestinians also have cultural traditions.
- Crying is no substitute for a substantial argument.
- Limit yourself only to phenomena that can be demonstrated by evidence.
- Remember: your opponents have feelings, too.
- Most people don't really like it when white kids scream racism.
- Being assiduously self-centered is an unappealing quality.
- Truth is a virtue.

EIGHT

On Being Palestinian and Other Things

What's this about my ethnic identity not being simply "Palestinian"? It's true. Intercontinental blood occupies my veins. This doesn't make me special. To the contrary, it makes me extraordinarily common. The only people espousing purity these days are either racist or deluded.

My father is Jordanian—or, as those who share his identity (he included) like to put it, *Jordanian* Jordanian. More than half of Jordan's citizens are of Palestinian origin, so people from the country sometimes clarify, if only by request, their ethnic identity (as opposed to "Jordanian" merely as a national designation). The apportioning of those identities into different categories is precarious because the locutions of nationhood arise from European colonization. Nevertheless, there now exists, however inchoate and delicate, a distinctly Jordanian kinship. It encompasses those who locate an origin on the East Bank of the River Jordan, in contradistinction to those in Jordan whose forebears occupied the West Bank (the Palestinians). The people on both sides of the river are deeply interconnected, but always maintained discrete identities.

(Hundreds of subcultures and affinities exist within and across each macro identity.)

These distinctions matter because Arabs aren't simply a mass of brown rabble that can be reduced to duplicate complexions. They also matter because some Zionist leaders propose transferring Palestinians to Jordan, a proposition that rationalizes ethnic cleansing while simultaneously erasing Jordanians.

The tensions between ethnic Palestinians and Jordanians are impossible to convey without serious attention to historical complexities, but tension does exist. In my case, constant reference to me as Palestinian or Palestinian American, of which I'm deeply proud, ignores an important component of my background. Like many proclamations of culture or nationality, these are political choices that stake belonging and geography to powerful articulations of rhetorical authority. I have no problem with this strategy, as the centering of Palestinians in conversations about decolonization is a necessary element of the nation-building project in Palestine. Moreover, I happily identify as Palestinian. Yet opposition to Israeli wrongdoing isn't exclusively the domain of Palestinians. It's important to enable people to access their own modes of identification.

I'm not merely a Jordanian/Palestinian hybrid, though. My mother was born and raised in Nicaragua, to immigrants from Ein Karem (now an Israeli area of West Jerusalem) and Beit Jala (adjacent to Bethlehem on the West Bank). Her sense of Arab identity is strong, but so is her attachment to Nicaragua. The Nicaraguan connection is important to me. I spent much time there during my early years, until my grandfather, a successful businessman, was displaced by the Sandinista Revolution. (Conversations between me and my mom around the issue of leftist revolutionaries in Latin American can be, um, animated.) After my grandparents settled in Honduras (which has a sizable Palestinian émigré population), I visited Tegucigalpa numerous times. My Spanish is better than my

Arabic. My great-grandfather Latinized his name from Bandy to Bandes. My ancestors are buried in Nicaragua. My mother cooks a killer hybrid of Central American and Levantine cuisine.

I also identify with my Appalachian upbringing. I'm often asked, with overwrought incredulity, how my parents ended up in Bluefield, a town in Southwest Virginia that shares a border with its twin city of Bluefield, West Virginia. There are lots of reasons, but the short version is that my father did graduate work at Virginia Tech, an hour east, and landed a job at the HBCU Bluefield State College. He and my mom thought Bluefield a good place for kids, so they stayed and raised three of them.

My relationship with Appalachia has always been complicated, but it was good for my burgeoning political consciousness. My family was subject to significant xenophobia—in some cases it would be fair to call it racism—but we also had access to neighborhoods and opportunities unavailable to African Americans. I realized at a young age that immigrants to the United States, even from the Arab World and Latin America, automatically supplant Black folk on the racial hierarchy, even if, as in Appalachia, they exist at considerable distance below white Christians.

Yet Appalachian culture—distinctive from Deep South folkways—has influenced my place in this world. I will never fully vacate the region no matter where I reside—nor do I have any desire to expunge Appalachia from my personhood. I don't have much of an accent, perhaps the most recognizable feature of the culture, but a consciousness of the landscape, with its elongated hills unfurling like the folds of an abandoned blanket, everywhere informs my sense of geography.

Finally, I have long been mistaken as Muslim. I am perfectly content to inhabit this identity, mind you, and in serious ways the peculiarities of my background render me at least culturally Islamic—or, as Edward Said put it, Islamicate. I am in fact Christian, however. Any Arab knows that with a first name of "Steven" I am unlikely Muslim; those schooled in religious tradition will further suspect, correctly, that I am Orthodox, to be specific.

When I proclaim to be Christian, it is with a flimsy relationship to Scripture or theology. I avoid setting foot in churches unless they are tourist attractions, and in such times I avoid the fountains of holy water. For me, it is a cultural and historical selfhood, an important one I cannot relinquish because in this case (as in all others) selfhood arises from association. For most descendants of the world's original Christian communities—Indigenous Christians, if you will—disavowing devotion or even belief in God isn't enough to surrender religious adjectives. I won't delete my history and my forebears for the prosaic opportunity to ingratiate myself to guardians of the unexamined sensibilities of Western modernity.

The iterations of an Indigenous Christianity are critical to the cultures and politics of the Arab World, especially Palestine, where Christ imagery pervades art and literature, and where Muslims hold the key to Jerusalem's Church of the Holy Sepulcher, built atop the crucifixion site of Golgotha. I'm uninterested in narratives that evoke ancient phenomena to rationalize ongoing acts of oppression. If he existed, Jesus was certainly Jewish—he's certainly Jewish in his mythological incarnation—but summoning the mythos of a doctrinal inheritance does little to clarify modern political claims. Whatever race or nationality one wants to attribute to Jesus, he lived in a land called Palestine. Thus his centrality to Palestinian culture.

Assuming all Arabs to be Muslim isn't always ignorance; it presupposes a civilizational binary that requires Islam to define a craven and undeveloped Arab mentality. The Arab Christian, then, undercuts a tidy (and brutish) understanding of the world, particularly if that Arab Christian shares an anti-imperialist outlook with Muslim compatriots.

I've experienced firsthand the importance to American patriots of maintaining simplistic categories of clashing cultures. My conflagration with UIUC isn't the first time I've been in trouble for political speech. In August 2013, entering what would become my final year at Virginia Tech, I wrote an article for *Salon* criticizing the omnipresence of the phrase "support our troops." (See Appendix Three.) Immediately upon publication of the piece, some readers disingenuously misread my thesis, with numerous groups, some located within the university, seeking to get me fired.

"I will fucking kill you if the opportunity presents itself you ungrateful motherfucker."

I shook my head as I forwarded this message, tucked entirely into the subject line, to the English Department chair at Virginia Tech. Then I went on to the next one. It was the day after the article had appeared. Not everybody was happy with my argument.

When I arrived at my office the following morning, a voicemail awaited: "I'm sure your son is a fucking faggot, just like you're a fucking faggot." (I offer the caller enormous benefit of the doubt by correctly transcribing the contraction.)

By that point, the vitriolic messages were arriving in my inbox faster than I could read them. I forwarded the death threats to the police and some of the funnier bluster to friends and family. I feared less for my life than for the well-being of a society in the thrall of this nationalistic furor—or at least a society made to genuflect to an all-American image of the flag lest anybody arouse that furor.

I don't genuflect. The first rule for any serious writer is to agitate the contentious and embrace the disreputable.

It didn't take long for the tenor of the messages to change. Suddenly I went from being a troop-hating fag to a jihadist, awash in the new vocabulary of apocalyptic struggle—*dhimmitude, swine, Taliban, anti-Semitism, Allah, terrorism, hijab, pederasty, oppressed women*—informing the limitless Clash of Civilizations.

"Moohamed was a murdering pig."

Apparently a bovine enthusiast, too, I thought as I clicked the message to make sure it contained only stupidity of the nonthreatening variety: "And so are you, all Muzzies are sub human dogs and should be put down like a diseased animal with Rabies. I only wish I lived in Virginia so i could hunt you down like the dog you are, I hope you die soon along with your family."

And so it went the rest of the day. (If you're wondering: no, one never becomes desensitized to racism.)

Just before slamming the lid of my laptop near midnight, I received a message on Facebook from a (white) high school friend I haven't seen in twenty years: "Man, I really don't think any of this would be happening if you were white." Some folks from my hometown (not in fact in the Islamoland of the hyperpatriot's imagination) had banished me from the right to be called a native son. But I grew up the child of immigrants in the heart of Southern Appalachia: my family was never accepted fully enough for banishment to mean anything.

The alignment of narratives was clear. Patriotism and ethnonationalism had again converged. There is nothing in the American past we can evoke for nostalgic coziness. Patriotism and ethnonationalism have always interacted in the United States.

My old classmate identified the correlation between race and the limits of acceptable critique, but is he correct that whiteness would have protected me from rage? In the abstract, no. Sean Penn has faced more rage than I can ever hope to elicit. Michael Moore isn't popular among flag-wavers, either. Nobody who conceptualizes patriotism or troop-worship as foolish will escape harsh feedback in today's United States.

Yet in the concrete, my old classmate's speculation is insightful. Whiteness cannot protect one from nationalistic wrath. White critics of patriotism and militarism may well be asked to leave the country. They may be ostracized for airing unpopular views. They may be called pussies and faggots. And they may be threatened with death. But their fundamental legitimacy as stewards of proper American-ness will rarely be questioned. It will instead be lamented as lapsed or forsaken. They will not field incessant questions about their religion (that is, whether or not they are Muslim). They will not be told to return to nations that don't exist (though they will be told to get out of this one).

In short, their dissidence will be conceptualized as individual failures, not as evidence of cultural deficiency.

My article about the trouble with the phrase "support the troops" suddenly had nothing to do with its own rhetorical anatomy. Instead, it became a referendum on the evils of Islam and the vileness of Arab culture.

Ethnonationalism and patriotism aren't identical, but they are often interchangeable. Dominant notions of patriotism in today's United States recycle the age-old assumption that the truest of all Americans, those who deserve the pleasure of abuse without accusations of atavistic disloyalty, are Christian, male, heterosexual, and white.

Scandinavians aren't fully white. The Irish aren't at all white. Neither are Italians. Jews are genetically nonwhite. Ukrainians are but dark-hearted impostors. Greeks and Spaniards are but a step away from being black.

At some point in American history, each of these statements was widely considered to be true. Somewhere along the way, each statement gave way to different truisms, depending on the social and political mood of the nation. Each community, in short, became at least white enough to escape the peripheries now inhabited by Latino/as, Arabs, Asians, and Muslims. (Blacks and Natives inhabit even more complex and insidious peripheries.)

American national identity has never been static, but its one constant is assimilation not into citizenship but into whiteness. The noun "American" is technically neutral, but its connotations rein-force whiteness as the default value of belonging. Patriotism is the natural culmination of this phenomenon. To express loyalty to a national ideal, one must accept the assumptions that provide the ideal its power. When those assumptions demand conformity to the rules of white normativity, they can seamlessly recirculate the racism endemic to narratives of American exceptionalism.

Are all patriotic folks therefore racist? No. In fact, it is possible to be both patriotic and antiracist. It is important to distinguish be-tween racism as an ethic, attitude, or philosophy and racism as a discourse transmitted through the broadcast of unexamined mythol-ogies. Transmitting those discourses may not bespeak personal ac-ceptance of racism, but it does bolster the institutions through which racism noiselessly affects the social order. Such is the tenacity of rac-ism; it perpetuates itself even in the absence of direct endorsement.

Sometimes, however, an event unleashes the racism hidden in the structures of patriotism. It happens, for instance, when an Arab is (mistakenly) seen to be criticizing "the troops," the most sacred trope of American pride.

I am not a fan of Barack Obama. Bank bailouts, kill lists, drone strikes, widespread torture—each policy is, in my opinion, unforgiv-able. But Barack Obama and I share something in common. We both experience the relentless wrath of Islamophobia without actu-ally being Muslim.

We are not alone. Islamophobes target those they wish to expel from the national identity they craft by maintaining the romance of a purer Americana. One need only be plausibly Muslim to become a target.

Obama has inspired a resurgence of ethnonationalism. No modern politician's ethnicity and religion have been so maligned, so mistrusted, as those of Obama, the heretical interloper, the untrue American. No birth certificate can overcome the aberrations of his

funny name and dark complexion. No level of diplomacy and conciliation can appease the anxiety of the hyperpatriots who bestow
on Obama a particular symbolism and then decry the decline of the
nation as a result of his symbolic incivility.

Rooting out evidence of people's foreignness has become such a
common way to argue that it overwhelms any critical analysis proffered by those perceived to be Muslim (by virtue of brown skin, an
unusual name, or distasteful headgear). Purveyors of this brand of
ethnonationalism are rarely called unpatriotic because they govern
the territories of normative American-ness. Patriotism is their domain, hostage to their definitional preferences.

In turn, patriotism is often a veiled lament at the changing
demographics of the United States. There is no space in the real
America for an alien president with socialist pathologies, immigrant hordes who undermine a timeless way of life, or an uppity
jihadist who denounces the nation's favorite platitude. By inces-
santly identifying and policing the limits of acceptable thought,
ethnonationalists conjoin patriotic demands with implicit racial
and sexual reproach (which periodically becomes explicit). This relentless shaming of dissidence benefits precisely two demographics:
politicians and their wealthy clientele.

We can spend energy formulating a more inclusive and
thoughtful patriotism, but ultimately it wouldn't be energy well
spent. Patriotism can only benefit all citizens if the state and its
institutions are inclusive of the entire populace. Until that happens,
and it has never happened in any epoch of American history, patriotism will have a stronger relationship with ethnonationalism than
with movements for equality.

In the meantime, we are stuck with this type of geopolitical
analysis, distilled from the most patriotic of the pundits to the be-
lieving viewers and finally into the inboxes of the infidels: "Do not
sit and mock this great country in defense of the violence-riddled,

sexual predatorial, Jihadist nations of Africa and Middle East, that you yearned to get away from."

Translation: as long as the far right remains in charge of defining patriotism and the liberal left continues reinforcing those definitions through weak-kneed appeals to tolerance, broader conversations about the state of our nation will be lazy, irrational, and violent—in other words, everything the current brand of patriotism asks us to be.

Hence the story of how I became Muslim by virtue of rejecting the racialized underpinnings of American exceptionalism. I do not, you will note, include "American" in my list of identities. I was born in the United States. I own an American passport. The moment we treat American-ness as anything grander, we reinforce hierarchies of belonging predicated on exclusion.

NINE

Spies (Don't) Like Us

At no time during the past century has discussion of academic freedom been dormant, which indicates that it's been at least a hundred years since being free of attack. Like most other concepts and practices, though, academic freedom works better when we complicate rather than venerate it.

Academic freedom is often a disturbance. It does not yet fully accommodate dissent. In many ways, academic freedom is a byproduct (and progenitor) of deeply conformist institutional cultures.[21] It can be an administrative convenience, a high-minded diversion, a shibboleth, or an appropriated symbol. Whatever it sometimes accomplishes or undermines, it is never pure.

Well before the McCarthy era, the most infamous period of restricted speech, academe was hostile to people of color, women, Jews, and queers. As Carol Smith illustrates in "The Dress Rehearsal for McCarthyism," the City College of New York purged numerous faculty, including Max Yergan, the first Black professor at any NYC public college, as a portent of the McCarthy era.[22]

---

21. For much more, read *The Imperial University: Academic Repression and Scholarly Dissent*, edited by Sunaina Maira and Piya Chatterjee (Minneapolis: University of Minnesota Press, 2014).

22. For a comprehensive analysis of faculty purges in New York City, see Marjorie

Nearly a century later, hostility toward these groups has not yet disappeared.

Similar cases precede mine at the University of Illinois, most recently James Kilgore, an instructor of global studies and urban planning who was dismissed—technically, his contract wasn't renewed, but it was a dismissal—when Kennedy learned of his prior role in the Symbionese Liberation Army. Many argue that Kilgore's past should disqualify him from teaching or that, as an untenured instructor, his employment is at the discretion of upper administration, but both views are mistaken. Kilgore's employment, as with all teachers, should be judged by his effectiveness in the classroom— that is, by the appropriateness and efficacy with which he educates students. Leaders of his home departments have discretion in determining his pedagogical quality and the need for the particular skillset he offers. No evidence indicates Kilgore is unfit to teach. It is not the role of the chairman of the board of trustees to intervene and impose top-down dicta. Kilgore is no longer a fugitive from the law; he spent the requisite time in prison for his crimes. Both empathy and protocol suggest that he exercise his right to make a living. Kilgore's detractors desire increased repression. They may not admit to that desire, but the arguments those detractors raise promote a repressive intervention they consider justified. I consider such concessions misguided. It's never a good idea to voluntarily cede power to our superiors.

Another interesting example is Bill Ayers, who, like Kilgore, has a colorful past in radical politics. Kennedy intervened in 2010 when Ayers came up for emeritus status (at the Chicago campus), which includes library privileges and a university email account and not much else, claiming that Ayers had once dedicated a book—1974's Weatherman Underground manifesto *Prairie Fire*—to Sirhan

---

Heins, *Priests of Our Democracy: The Supreme Court, Academic Freedom, and the Anti-Communist Purge* (New York: NYU Press, 2013).

Sirhan, the assassin of Kennedy's father, Bobby. Kennedy argued that "there can be no place in a democracy to celebrate political assassinations or to honor those who do so." The problem with this argument is that Ayers hadn't celebrated or honored Sirhan Sirhan. *Prairie Fire* is dedicated to Harriett Tubman and John Brown, along with all political prisoners. An artist's montage included the names of hundreds of political prisoners, among them Sirhan Sirhan. Ayers's situation looks very little like mine but in one important respect: the interference of the board of trustees in an academic matter.

Of interest is the following line from Kennedy's statement on his decision regarding Ayers: "I am aware of the thoughtfulness of the great educator John Henry Newman who believed that a university should be not only a place of sharp discourse but also, ultimately, a place of civility." The reliance by the University of Illinois on civility as a form of castigation predates my termination. Kennedy affirms the usefulness of sharp discourse, but immediately subsumes it to the need for civility, which is the paramount goal of the university. The passage reads as both duplicity and ultimatum.

Leo Koch provides the most illuminating example. An assistant professor of biology, Koch was fired in 1960 for publishing a letter in the *Daily Illini* that challenged repressive sexual mores, decrying "the widespread crusades against obscenity." Hysteria ensued, with university president David Dobbs Henry declaring the letter "offensive and repugnant" and eventually dismissing Koch. The board upheld the dismissal. A local reverend had led a pressure campaign on Henry, smearing Koch as a communist and predator. The Illinois Supreme Court and the Supreme Court of the United States declined to intervene. Three years later the AAUP censured UIUC. Koch went on to cofound the Sexual Freedom League in New York City. He never again taught college.

While the differences between my case and Koch's are apparent—era, subject matter, discipline, rank, tenure status—there is significant overlap. The president and board acted arbitrarily, ignoring faculty governance and interjecting themselves in the academic side of the university. Koch had no due process. An outside pressure campaign existed. The university fired Koch for an extramural utterance. Powerful interest groups were offended. Moral sensibility prevailed over intellectual inquiry. Upper administration claimed to be protecting the students. The case became a media sensation. Ironically, had Koch criticized Israel in 1960, and had I condemned sexual puritanism in 2014, neither of us would have been fired. The topic is less important than the system.

Folks frequently compare my situation with those of Ward Churchill and Norman Finkelstein. Both lost their jobs because of political speech and massive pressure campaigns, but here too there are crucial differences. Churchill, for example, didn't technically get fired for speech, but for academic misconduct. That sort of charge never would have been investigated had Churchill not proffered controversial statements, but in his case the University of Colorado hedged against (illegal) breaches of academic freedom by pursuing a strategy that might allow it to justify the dismissal of a tenured professor. A jury found the university's claims of misconduct invalid, but the court didn't allow Churchill to regain his job.

Finkelstein did lose his job at DePaul University explicitly because of speech—more specifically, speech critical of Israel—but it came in the form of tenure denial rather than termination from a tenured position. On a personal level, the distinction would matter little, if at all, to Finkelstein, whose academic career was destroyed. Indeed, on a personal level, his situation is similar to mine.[23] The fact of tenured status in my firing, though, adds a legal dimension portending an even greater rollback of academic freedom. One of the problems of tenure is that if a scholar fails to earn it she loses her job, a problem afflicted by the sensitivities of majoritarianism. In the

---

23. Future GRE analogy: Dershowitz is to Finkelstein as Nelson is to Salaita.

past decade, dozens of women of color have failed to achieve tenure despite excellent dossiers. Tenure can suppress just as effectively as it can protect.

We can point to recent cases of orchestrated harassment that didn't end in dismissal, though those cases occupied inordinate personal energies and resulted in damaged reputations. William Robinson, professor of sociology at UC-Santa Barbara, endured a months-long campaign of threats and suppression because he refused to "repent"—an actual demand—for sharing articles about Israel's 2009 Gaza slaughter, Operation Cast Lead.[24] Pro-Israel groups, with the complicity of UCSB and UC System administrators, accused Robinson of "anti-Semitism" and of violating the Faculty Code of Conduct, the technicality they hoped would lead to a legal opening for termination, a là the Churchill case.

Five years later, Robinson reflected on his ordeal:

> The persecution to which I was subjected involved a litany of harassment, slander, defamation of character and all kinds of threats against the university by outside forces if I was not dismissed, as well as hate mail and death threats from unknown sources. More insidiously, it involved a shameful collaboration between a number of university officials and outside forces from the Israel lobby as the university administration stood by silently, making a mockery of academic freedom.

A few things stand out in Robinson's passage. First, we again see the

---

24. Now that I'm in need of a job, perhaps the IDF will hire me to name its war crimes. A few suggestions: Operation Dersh (when claiming to support a Palestinian state while building settlements on that state's land); Operation Idiotic Goyim (when using phrases like "telegenically dead" just isn't enough); Operation Because God Said So (self-explanatory); Operation Secure the Two Feet of Northeastern Perimeter Apartheid Wall Currently Susceptible to Banksy Graffiti (because it sounds much better than "protective edge"); Operation Defend Defensive Defending of Defense (more subtlety, please); Operation Blame Hamas for Everything from Hadassah to the Leaky Sink in That One Bathroom in the Knesset (because Hamas).

reliance by pro-Israel groups on the minutiae of procedure, which ignores the macro-level protections of academic freedom. Where those groups cannot win with the dissemination of ideas, they scour procedural opportunities to punish political antagonists. Israeli author Manfred Gerstenfeld promoted this type of strategy in the *Jerusalem Post*:

> A number of scholars are also sloppy with their footnotes and may quote from incorrect or poor sources. If a scholar has many footnotes as references, the risk of a significant number of mistakes increases. Once one has a list of those university lecturers who support the boycott of Israel, one can select targets among them for investigation. It is likely that if one chooses one's targets intelligently, one would find a few who plagiarize, publish using incorrect sources or are guilty of academic fraud. It is also likely that some of their colleagues would gladly provide the names of those to be investigated. The lecturers that do not meet academic standards would then be exposed within their universities and among their professional colleagues. One only has to find a few such cases in order to greatly diminish the threat of boycotts.

According to this vision of collegiality, every colleague is a potential spy and any mistaken citation should result in destruction of reputation or livelihood.

Robinson's antagonists performed the strategy. Rather than protecting a distinguished faculty member, UCSB administrators entertained the pressure groups—sadly, a common occurrence in cases that involve criticism of Israel. They secretly hosted a meeting with Anti-Defamation League executive director Abraham Foxman. Had an attendee of that meeting not revealed Foxman's presence, it would presumably remain a secret. Robinson attributes his survival in large part to the organizing efforts of graduate and undergraduate students, another example of the schism between grassroots versus top-down power when it comes to Israel-Palestine.

Joseph Massad's ordeal at Columbia University was similar to

Robinson's experience, but it lasted far longer and included an intensity of viciousness unusual even around the issue of Palestine. The David Project and other pro-Israel operations targeted Massad for the usual charges of indoctrination, anti-Semitism, aggressiveness, intolerance, and bullying. Here the specter of classroom suitability surfaces, a common and underhanded aspersion. Massad's response was quite like the ones I've been forced to offer:

> I am dedicated to all my students, many of whom are Jewish. Neither Columbia University nor I have ever received a complaint from any student claiming intimidation or any such nonsense. Students at Columbia have many venues of lodging complaints, whether with the student deans and assistant deans, school deans and assistant deans, department chairmen, departmental directors of undergraduate studies, the ombudsman's office, the provost, the president, and the professors themselves. No such complaint was ever filed. Many of my Jewish and non-Jewish students (including my Arab students) differ with me in all sorts of ways, whether on politics or on philosophy or theory. This is exactly what teaching and learning are about, how to articulate differences and understand other perspectives while acquiring knowledge, how to analyze one's own perspective and those of others, how to interrogate the basis of an opinion.

I don't feel the need to rehearse Massad's story—eventually he earned tenure despite relentless obstacles—except to say that I admire his fortitude and intelligence and try my best to emulate his example. Reading about the sorry state of his tenure case reminds me of the forces I (and, more frequently, my allies) now battle.

Like Massad, I am an Arab—though, unlike Massad, I am not an immigrant to the United States. Nevertheless, our ethnic subjectivities closely relate. Am I suggesting that ethnicity plays a role in how these modes of attack develop, how discursive strategies emerge based on the identity of the target, and how corporate media discuss the resultant controversies? That's exactly what I suggest.

The differences are visible.

For Arab or Muslim critics of Israel, longstanding Orientalist bromides enact outrage and then command media narratives. Those bromides include our inability or unwillingness to be refined; our reliance on emotion rather than logic; our genetic tendency to dislike Jews; our atavistic inclinations to violence; our natural lack of objectivity; our tenuous ability to comprehend the customs of modernity; and our threat to the well-being of civilized geographies. While the Jewish anti-Zionist faces accusations of self-hatred and racial treason, the Arab or Muslim counterpart implicates and thus must exculpate an entire culture. Massad and I weren't tasked with defending ourselves, but the very humanity of the Palestinian people.

The cases I mention indicate that nowadays the most visible site of debate around academic freedom is the Israel-Palestine conflict, in particular as it is approached through BDS, though this site of debate is in dialogue with broader questions of racism and colonization. Academic boycott of Israel, specifically, has become a passionate topic on campus. Since the ASA resolution, BDS also has been discussed passionately off campus.

Let's look at the praxis accompanying the discussion. Those against academic boycott, both on and off campus, consistently invoke academic freedom as the reasoning for their position (though some confess loyalty to Israel as a motivation). A boycott, the argument goes, would restrict the academic freedom of Israeli students and researchers and impinge on the exchange of ideas so crucial to scholarly life.

Numerous writers have consistently unmasked this assertion as fallacious. Academic boycott is careful to distinguish between institutions and individuals. Some have observed that the distinction is functionally impossible, but only individuals who consciously participate in advocacy for the Israeli state would be affected. Boycott transfers responsibility to the individual, but never targets her for preemptive exclusion. In this sense academic boycott is consummately reactive.

There is scant evidence that academic boycott systematically limits an Israeli scholar's ability to travel and conduct research.[25] On the other hand, engagement with Palestine has repeatedly proved deleterious to one's professional development. In the months following the ASA resolution, hundreds of college and university presidents released condemnatory statements, usually without consulting the folks on campus on whose behalf they purported to speak. Their statements invariably deified the sanctity of academic freedom, but no college or university president has yet criticized UIUC. We can never adequately understand academic freedom if we don't first dislodge it from the venerable rites of rhetorical hypocrisy.

An aging collection of malcontents lionized the AAUP when it condemned academic boycott, but recoiled when the organization criticized the University of Illinois.[26] Such opportunists adulate the fascistic minutiae of procedure. The ASA, they bellowed, suffered procedural irregularities, despite the fact that the process for the boycott resolution was more exacting than any other in the association's history. It included a membership vote that overwhelmingly supported boycott. (The membership vote was added to mollify half a dozen grousers.) The only intellectual transaction such critics sincerely oppose is the procedure of decolonization. They have no stable values beyond a desire to protect Israel from criticism. Every desperate attempt at principle is merely a strategy toward this end.

---

25. See further *Against Apartheid: The Case for Boycotting Israeli Universities*, edited by Ashley Dawson and Bill V. Mullen (Chicago: Haymarket Books, 2015).

26. Said Jonathan Marks in an attempt to make the AAUP more palatable to Israel's natural allies on the far right: "There has been some bad blood between the AAUP and more conservative groups, like the National Association of Scholars, that also oppose boycotts. Readers may judge NAS president Peter Wood's attack on the AAUP for themselves. But, regardless of whether Wood is right that the AAUP is changing for the worse, AAUP stalwarts like Reichman, Cary Nelson, and Ernst Benjamin have led the charge against boycotts. Whatever the AAUP's defects may be, we should probably join them (can someone loan me $147?), even if we sometimes must sometimes disagree with or criticize them."

The ASA resolution has no ability to abrogate academic freedom even if that were its intent. It wouldn't be fair to reduce the resolution to symbolism, but it doesn't possess regulatory discrepancy. The ASA has never had formal relationships with Israeli institutions, so there is nothing to sever. The resolution merely formalizes extant practices. Neither can the ASA leadership annul anybody's membership for violating the terms of academic boycott. Any ASA member can travel to, say, Tel Aviv University and pal around with racists and war criminals. And anybody can come from Israel to attend the ASA convention (they do each year). The resolution supersedes symbolism because it orients specific policies: the ASA will not hold a meeting in West Jerusalem or invite a representative of the Israeli consulate to deliver a keynote. It does nothing to limit the prerogatives of individual ASA members, however.

A central contribution of these boycott resolutions has been to illustrate why academic freedom should be trained on those who have been punished for speech or advocacy rather than retaining its typical posture in service of the oppressor. Academic boycott never acts on a person's expression of views, but on his actions. Does he perform at the behest of the government of Israel? If so, he is actively participating in the subjugation of Palestinian students and scholars and thus subject to boycott. In short, boycott is not a contravention of academic freedom, but an expression of it. Given the reliance by pro-Israel campaigners on government and the elite to regulate speech, along with the punitive measures taken against BDS proponents, it is clear which side presents a legitimate threat to academic freedom.

Often lost in arguments about BDS is a fundamental question: what of the Palestinians? Their rights to speech, assembly, and organizing, in both Israel and the Occupied Territories, are severely limited, in many cases nonexistent. Far from shutting down scholarly interchange, boycott implicates institutions whose practices suppress the academic freedom of an entire class of people.

BDS, then, is a terrific framework for approaching academic freedom as a discourse above and beyond its functional role, which has never been comprehensive. Discursively, academic freedom can easily rationalize dispossession of rights, in the same way that conservative politicians expropriate the vocabulary of civil rights to conceptualize white men as the true victims of American racism. For this reason (among others), I'm tepid about academic freedom as a right. I consider it more productive to think about academic freedom as an idea constantly in flux, whose practice is not always aligned with its ideals.

The preservation of academic freedom as a rights-based structure, in other words, shouldn't be the focus of our work. We should focus on the development and maintenance of just labor conditions and the disengagement of our institutions from the exercise of state violence. Academic freedom is important insofar as it protects our ability to do this work. When it doesn't offer such protection, then it becomes just another exalted slogan, the type many administrators evoke to conceal the ugly side of university governance.

To put it in simpler terms, we shouldn't trust "academic freedom." We do better to apply to the term the same scrutiny we direct at the phenomena we study, a process academic freedom supposedly insulates from recrimination. Only when academic freedom is sufficiently anatomized can it perform its inherent promise.

Academic freedom intersects with constitutional free speech, but the two aren't coterminous. Free speech, in its most distilled version, is a legal protection against governmental recrimination. It affirms the right of assembly and public expression, but has little standing in the private workplace; employers are free to terminate workers who articulate words or viewpoints anathema to management. Those protections have never been consistently enforced, or comprehensive. The advent of "free speech zones" and other spatial limitations of expression complicate both the function and philosophy of the first amendment.

Academic freedom and free speech both inform the mythologies of the liberal state. Authorities and activists often uphold them in context of an exceptionalist view of American modernity. Academic freedom and free speech, then, are implicated in the exclusionary practices of the US imperium. They are central to a particular self-image of linear progress.

In January 2014, a polar vortex descended on much of the United States. Amid blistering cold in Champaign-Urbana, Wise decided to hold classes as usual. On Twitter, many students reacted to this decision with sexist and racist invective, under the hashtag #FuckPhyllis. (Wise is of Chinese origin.) Choosing not to take action against the offending students, Wise noted that "the negative comments, as offensive as they were, are protected speech."

Wise's response has become another canonical example of free speech as sacrosanct to American identity, along with the KKK marching through Jewish neighborhoods in Skokie, Illinois, and the Supreme Court upholding the right of Fred Phelps and his Westboro Baptist Church to protest a serviceperson's funeral. These are the actions of a state confident in the vitality of its liberal values.

But what about the folks who attack those liberal values and the colonial histories from which they emerge?

Free speech is less malleable for those who condemn state power. Critiquing excess is often acceptable, but not the values of capitalism that deem excess chivalrous or desirable. The list of academics affected by these recurrent dragnets is distinguished: Chandler Davis, Staughton Lynd, Howard Zinn, Angela Davis, Sami Al-Arian, Bertrand Russell. Hundreds of scholars of color have simply been denied tenure. Hundreds more never got jobs in the first place.

We think of tenure as protection of those who undertake political engagement, but tenure contains an inverse: through its denial, or the threat of its denial, it can fundamentally restrict political engagement.

TEN

PeP Talk

A common appellation to describe liberal Zionists is PeP: Progressive except for Palestine. This jagged acronym applies to people who profess to oppose racism, sexism, imperialism, war, segregation, dogma, meanness, and incivility, but who suddenly become quite less enlightened vis-à-vis Israel, or who torture their ethics in risible contortions in order to render support for Israel compatible with their progressive self-image.

PeP has served us well, but it's ready to be retired. It doesn't adequately describe a problem that has more to do with histrionics than with inconsistency or hypocrisy.

I don't oppose catchy acronyms, though, so allow me to propose an alternative: RbI, Regressive because of Israel. This formulation proposes that regressiveness rather than progressiveness be the default identification of those who lionize Israel. It's an ethical proposition in addition to a rhetorical one: consciousness is defined most acutely by its willingness to accommodate colonial violence.

Apologism for Israel, in short, isn't an aberration. It merely illuminates the aberrant.

ELEVEN

Palestine in the American Imagination

To fully understand the phenomena of colonial logic and academic freedom, especially in relation to the Middle East, it's useful to examine Palestine as it connects to notions of Indigeneity in North America, in particular the place of Palestine in the American imagination.

I mean three things by "imagination," though the term lends itself to infinite possibilities.

1. How Palestine has been *imagined* in American discourses since the early days of European settlement. That is to say, how it has been invented as a mythological space based largely on the desires of the American polity.

2. How Palestine, in its biblical incarnations, provided early settlers an ideal of nationhood that continues to influence American identity, and even its foreign policy.

3. How Palestine has been constructed by American politicians and commentators as a site of intractable struggle, a symbol of a particular sort of premodernity that creates anxiety around the inability of the American ideal to fully actualize.

Palestine has been as crucial to the making of America—itself a contested and inconsistent space—as any other landscape, including those in Africa that provided slave labor and the nostalgic reconstruction of the mother countries, England, Germany, Italy, Ireland, and so forth. In other words, although the United States has been embroiled in Palestine only recently, within the past hundred years, Palestine as a myth and an avatar informs the groundwork of the American project. Palestine is the progenitor of Manifest Destiny.

Here's a passage from Puritan firebrand Cotton Mather, speaking in the early eighteenth century: "Turn not your back till they are consumed. Wound them that they shall not be able to arise. And for a close, let me remind you, that while you fight, we'll pray. . . . We will keep in the Mount with our hands lifted up, while you are in the field with your lives in your Hands against the Amalek that is now annoying this Israel in the wilderness."

The pronoun "they" refers to the Native tribes Mather wanted exterminated, as was the Indigenous population of the Holy Land, on orders from God, as recorded in the Old Testament's Book of Joshua. Amalek is a reference to the land of Canaan and its environs, occupied by numerous tribes. Mather, like other Puritans, superimposes a biblical narrative onto the American landscape. The settlers are Israel in the wilderness; the Natives are godless souls—Canaanites, Amalekits, Jebusites, Hittites, and others who must be removed or slaughtered in order for a divine vision to prevail. In one sense, Mather's discourse is an allegory; in a very real way, though, he was being literal in describing his circumstances as a New World settler.

Mather, by the way, famously referred to Natives as "the accursed seed of Canaan."[27] Mather wasn't an outlier. His narrative of American settlement as a holy enterprise reflects a discourse, with variations, used for centuries in the process of New World conquest,

---

27. There is some question as to whether Mather actually made this statement, but it certainly seems like something he would have said.

even among the secular. Indians inhabited Amalek; settlers were to tame the wilderness and create a Godly kingdom of milk and honey.

What does this have to do with modern Palestine? Lots, actually. Palestinians are conceptualized in significant American demographics as a newfangled Amalek preventing the establishment, or reestablishment, of a mandatory holy state. Scholars generally call this type of viewpoint messianism. The United States has long been a deeply messianic nation.

This messianism isn't limited to practices of settlement, nor does it adhere to tidy liberal-conservative binaries. Martin Luther King, Jr. used messianic discourses in his speeches and essays. So did George W. Bush. Look at the number of towns in the United States named Canaan or New Canaan. There are lots of Bethlehems and Hebrons and Palestines. Just as there are countless place names derived from Native languages. The interactions of biblical narrative and Native peoplehood help define Americana.

The Exodus narrative on which so many versions of colonial salvation and liberation theology are based is a terrific model of freedom from oppression: an ethnic minority population is enslaved in a foreign land. It relies on its wit, morality, perseverance, courage, and, most of all, Godly assistance, to seek a promised land of excess and independence.

It wasn't such a terrific model to the tribes already in the Holy Land, however. They were slaughtered at the behest of God. That is to say, they were victims of another group's liberation. A famous essay by Robert Warrior makes this point. Called "Canaanites, Cowboys, and Indians: A Native American Perspective," in it Warrior observes,

> The [Exodus] narrative tells us that the Canaanites have status only as the people Yahweh removes from the land in order to bring the chosen people in. They are not to be trusted, nor are they to be allowed to enter into social relationships with the people of Israel. They are wicked and their religion is to be avoided at all costs. The laws put forth regarding strangers and sojourners

may have stopped the people of Yahweh from wanton oppression, but presumably only after the land was safely in the hands of Israel. The covenant of Yahweh depends on this.

For this reason, comparison of Natives and Palestinians has flourished in recent years. Both groups occupy the regrettable position of unchosen in narratives of Godly conquest. The Holy Land accompanied American colonization. The United States has returned the favor in its support of Israel. The centrality of messianism and Manifest Destiny to American national identity ensures that many Americans will identify with Israel seemingly on impulse (though impulses are never as neutral or natural as they pretend to be). To identify with Israel is in many ways to accept the mythologies of American conquest.

Steven Newcomb explores these phenomena in his book, *Pagans in the Promised Land*. He notes that "when dominating forms of reasoning (categorization) found in the Old Testament narrative are unconsciously used to reason about American Indians, Indian lands metaphorically become—from the viewpoint of the United States—the promised land of the chosen people of the United States." Newcomb's analysis is valuable, though I would question the extent to which reasoning about American Indians as biblical Canaanites is unconscious. The teleology of North America as a new promised land is obvious in the early days of European settlement, but even now the inventions of America as a metaphorical Israel, with Indians as a romanticized but ungodly presence, remains common—quite consciously so.

Let me talk a little about modern Palestine, because, as with most aspects of history, it's difficult, if not impossible, to understand the past without making sense of the present. Here are some basic facts about the Israel-Palestine conflict:

- Israel currently occupies the Palestinian West Bank and Syrian Golan Heights in contravention of international law. It exerts full control over the Gaza Strip. At various points in its history, it occupied the Egyptian Sinai Peninsula and southern Lebanon (some say it still does).

- West Bank Palestinians are subject to a set of discriminatory laws, as are Israel's Palestinian citizens.
- Israel's military occupation is illegal according to international law and various human rights conventions.
- Israel displaced around 700,000 (perhaps as many as 800,000) Palestinians during the period of its founding, 1947–49.
- Israel has killed more than a thousand children in the past decade.
- Israel considers itself a state for all Jews, anywhere in the world, rather than one for its actual citizens.
- Israel is required by international law to evacuate the West Bank and Golan Heights.
- Israel is the sole nuclear power in the Middle East.
- Israel receives $3 billion in annual aid from the United States, give or take a couple hundred million.
- There is unassailable documentary evidence that from the earliest days of Zionism its leaders intended to cleanse the native Arab population from Palestine.[28]

I selected these facts from a Rolodex of possibilities. Anybody can pick and choose issues to supplement or create a particular story, so facts are never in themselves indicators of truth. From the Palestinian point of view, though, the items I mention are crucial. They comprise the historical circumstances by which Palestinians have been dispossessed.

---

28. Vladimir Jabotinsky was the most straightforward early Zionist: "It is of no importance whether we quote Herzl or Herbert Samuel to justify our activities. Colonization itself has its own explanation, integral and inescapable, and understood by every Arab and every Jew with his wits about him. Colonization can have only one goal. For the Palestinian Arabs this goal is inadmissible. This is in the nature of things. To change that nature is impossible."

I also highlight them as a counterpoint to modern Palestine in the American imagination. As in the past, Palestine is a symbol. For many, it signals Arab and Muslim barbarity and a key battleground in the global war on terror. For others, it is a space of courageous resistance. On the political left especially, Palestine has become a metaphor of liberatory action, the site of a new Third World struggle against Western imperialism. For others still, it is a confounding example of tribal or religious intractability.

Palestine exists along (or creates) numerous fault lines in American political discourse. In many ways, Israel is a fuller realization of the American dream. Palestine, on the other hand, is an anxiety, one whose existence ensures the survival of the American Indian. It is also a geography where myth and matter converge. Even though there are serious geopolitical implications in Israel and Palestine for the United States, Americans are engaged in the so-called Holy Land for reasons that eclipse geopolitics.

In turn, arguments about the Israel-Palestine conflict can be messy. People feel so invested because the conflict is a matter of identity just as much as it is of geography and economics.

Yet I'd like to propose that Israel-Palestine is no more intense or unusual than any other violent conflict over land. We confer to it an exceptional status, but when we remove the mythology (which, admittedly, is hard to do) it's just another case of settler colonization, not terribly unlike what happened in North America, Algeria, South Africa, New Zealand, and Australia. The conflict is easily understood and has a straightforward solution: it began because one group of people forcibly settled the land of another group of people. Its solution is to stop the colonization and implement democracy for all citizens rather than a tiered system of access and belonging based on religious background. A solution is "complex" or "impossible" only for those invested in the illegal occupation of Palestine and the iniquity it produces.

It's also so complex and impossible because in the United States settlement is seen as normative, inevitable, and irreversible. I can't count the times I've heard some variation of this argument: "The dispossession of Palestinians happened and as tragic as it was we're all better off because of it. Look at the United States: it had to displace Indians to create the world's greatest democracy. Should the United States return stolen land to the Indians?"

This argument assumes that history is irreversible, but such a notion can only be put forward by the victor, who, after all, spent plenty of time reversing history in order to accrue his power. The most important thing about its logic is what it tells us about ourselves, what it says about our acceptance, if only unconsciously, of profound violence in the service of democracy.

The question "should the United States return stolen land to the Indians?" is rhetorical, of course; the answer is embedded in the question, whose point is to emphasize an obvious absurdity. The correlation is that it would be absurd for Israel to do the same for the Palestinians. It's a mutual delegitimization of native populations. But the question can't function in isolation; it relies on a sweep of history that illuminates how crucial the mythologies of Palestine are to the American imagination.

Israeli historian Benny Morris puts it this way: "Even the great American democracy couldn't come to be without the forced extinction of Native Americans. There are times the overall, final good justifies terrible, cruel deeds."

This reasoning suggests a finality to the past, an affirmation of tragedy trapped in the immutability of linear time. Its logic is terribly cliché, a peculiar form of common sense always taken up, everywhere, by the beneficiaries of colonial power.

The problems with invoking Native American genocide to rationalize Palestinian dispossession are legion. The most noteworthy problem speaks to the unresolved detritus of American history:

Natives aren't objects of the past; they are living communities whose numbers are growing. It's rarely a good idea to ask rhetorical questions that have literal answers. Yes, the United States absolutely should return stolen land to the Indians. That's precisely what its treaty obligations require it to do.

The United States is a settler nation, but its history hasn't been settled. Many people invoke Natives as if they lost a contest that entrapped them in the past—and this only if Natives are considered at all. As a result, most analyses of both domestic and foreign policies are inadequate, lacking a necessary context of continued colonization and resistance.

For Natives, political aspirations aren't focused on accessing the mythologies of a multicultural America, but on the practices of sovereignty and self-determination, consecrated in treaty agreements (and in their actual histories). Treaties aren't guidelines or suggestions; they are nation-to-nation agreements whose stipulations exist in perpetuity. That the federal government still ignores so many of those agreements indicates that colonization is not simply an American memory.

One of the most famous violations is the Treaty of Fort Laramie (1851, 1868), which guaranteed the Lakota possession of the Black Hills. The American government seized the Black Hills nine years after signing the treaty, in 1877, having discovered sizable deposits of gold and other precious minerals.

In 1980, the US Supreme Court ruled that the federal government had unjustly appropriated the Black Hills (the ruling doesn't use the word "stolen," but it's an accurate descriptor of what occurred). The court awarded the Lakota $15.5 million (now well over $100 million with inflation) for the adjusted value of the appropriated land, but the tribe has consistently refused the monetary settlement, preferring instead to retain entitlement to its historic territory.

To clarify: vast portions of five US states—North Dakota, South Dakota, Nebraska, Wyoming, and Montana—are Indian land according to a treaty to which the American government voluntarily assented. The highest legal authority in the United States has acknowledged that a significant portion of the land in question is rightfully Lakota. The American government refuses to return that land.

A comparable example of continuing US colonization (unfortunately, this could go on a while) exists in Hawaii, the youngest American state. Hawaii became an American possession in 1893 due to a coup d'état led by colonist Sanford Dole, cousin of James Dole, who, not so coincidentally, made a fortune growing produce on the islands.

President Grover Cleveland commissioned an investigation into the overthrow of the Hawaiian monarchy, led by Georgia congressman James Henderson Blount. The Blount Report condemned the annexation of Hawaii. The condemnation ultimately did no good. American businessmen and politicians saw too much value in the new property to constrain their avarice. To this day, the Kanaka Maoli (Native Hawaiians) do not recognize the legitimacy of the annexation and consider themselves subjects of foreign rule. While American tourists enjoy hula dances and Mai Tais on stolen land, the Kanaka Maoli, victims of a conquest that in no way has passed, continue to organize for liberation.

Colonialism is present across North America in less obvious ways, though the lack of obviousness doesn't mitigate its relevance. Corporate malfeasance is especially harmful to Indigenous communities in the Americas (and across the world). Native nations have dealt with an uninterrupted expropriation of resources for over a century and now experience an inordinate amount of disease and pollution. At present, Natives and their allies in both Canada and the United States are working to stop the Keystone XL Pipeline, a project that portends environmental damage and serious health concerns.

Natives have encountered violence in attempting to exercise their hunting and fishing rights. (Does the phrase "save a fish, spear an Indian" ring a bell?)[29] Police brutality is acute in Indian Country. Natives, women especially, are murdered at an epidemic rate, with the majority of cases unresolved. And many communities are still waiting on various institutions to comply with federal legislation requiring the return of artifacts and human remains to their rightful owners.

Nor should we forget that the forced sterilization of Native women and the kidnapping of children to be educated (read: brutally assimilated) in government boarding schools, where many were sexually molested and subject to countless other abuses, were still happening within the past half-century.[30]

The inveterate omission of these realities in analyses of American politics constitutes an erasure of Indigenous histories and illuminates why it is so easy to conceptualize the United States as historically settled. If we recall the existence of dynamic Indian nations, though, we have no choice but to rethink the commonplaces of American virtue.

It is a foolish conceit to suggest that history has ended in the United States. No amount of ignorance (willful or unwitting) will invalidate the vigorous efforts to decolonize the North and South American continents. Decolonization doesn't mean kicking Americans and Canadians out of their homes. It means, among other things, that Indigenous peoples retain or regain stewardship of their ancestral lands and don't exist as wards of the federal government. Decolonization supersedes mere implementation of treaty rights. It demands the survival of Indigenous ways of being.

When Israel's supporters invoke the dispossession of living communities as a rationale for colonizing Palestine, they betray a profound

---

29. This is the "nice" version. "Save a fish, spear a squaw" was also popular.
30. Neither should we forget that Israel was recently busted for sterilizing African immigrants.

disdain of Indigenous humanity, the sort of contempt that renders the oppressor's psyche so unsettled. They also illustrate that far from being the dialogical opposite of Third World barbarism, modernity itself is impossible without violent practices justified as inevitable.

Two observations suffice to connect these matters to Palestine:

1. Limiting Israel-Palestine to religious acrimony or to the code words of terrorism and democracy misses the point. Badly. Whatever our viewpoint, we should treat the conflict as familiar and unexceptional, as something that doesn't mystify reality, but informs it.

And

2. I urge us to extract Palestine from the American imagination and think about it in the context of its own lived experience instead.

Everything I just discussed contextualizes my situation with the University of Illinois. That I was hired to teach in American Indian Studies is crucial because my termination isn't simply a personal problem, but a representation of the marginal standing of American Indian and Indigenous Studies (and the humanities and social sciences more broadly). That university administrators deployed the language of civility in the wake of its decision illuminates a model of governance deeply rooted in colonial ethos.

Civility exists in the lexicon of conquest. It is the language of Cotton Mather's diatribes. It is the discourse of educated racism. It is the sanctimony of the authoritarian. It is the pretext of the oppressor.

To support Palestine in the American polity automatically entails an act of radicalism, no matter how measured or demonstrable the point of view. It is necessarily uncivil, no matter how cordial the appeal. To raise this support in context of Native peoples is doubly threatening and requires a special administrative reaction. It recalls periods of American history that supposedly have ended, that have no place in a modern consciousness, but continue to nag and persist.

It would be a great mistake to conceptualize my termination as having much to do with me beyond the unpredictability of chance.

I and UIUC are merely antagonists in a broader contest about how universities will function in the future. They can continue to be neoliberal corporations or they can reclaim their status as sites of actual education. We are all entrapped by the history of civility as a rationale for violence and a rhetorical device to neatly separate the modern from the savage.

Throughout this history, academic freedom has never been a panacea. In too many instances African Americans have been brutalized by the pieties of objectivity. The same is true of Indigenous peoples and of any deviant body or body of deviant ideas. Adjunct faculty have no functional academic freedom. Upper administrators aren't swelling the ranks of contingent faculty just to save money; they desire a workforce that can be expendable and easily punished if that's what the political winds demand.

Of course this is all about civility. Civility is not a state of mind. It is a regime. Civility reinforces the conceits of modernity. Academic freedom is a function of modernity. It will therefore always have difficulty accommodating systematic critique of state power. No state attaches more power to the stature of its identity than Israel. The United States is inseparable from Israeli power. This is the context of my situation with the University of Illinois.

There is a semiotics of disputation at play here. People feel invested in the outcome of that situation because its implications inform the corporatization of academe and the erosion of democratic governing practices on campus. The images of Palestine in the American imagination facilitate this decline of democracy. The continued occupation of Indian Country means the democracy never fulfilled its own self-image.

My firing deeply affected the American Indian Studies Program. Beyond the fact that the department selected me from a national search by adhering to regular hiring procedures, which entail a tremendous amount of work, its faculty have been relentlessly vilified by the administration's supporters. The entrenched anti-Indian racism of UIUC found yet another pretext for its existence. Majoritarian anger at the world found its scapegoat, as it does so often, in the nagging figure of the Native.

Management's acolytes all over the Internet accused Warrior, who is director of UIUC's American Indian Studies Program, of nepotism because he served on my dissertation committee at the University of Oklahoma. It was a thoroughly dishonest accusation. It's perfectly normal in a small field like AIS for somebody to end up in the same department as one of her mentors. Denying this simple reality is another example of ethnonationalists being unwilling to acknowledge that their support of Israel overrides whatever principles they might otherwise maintain.

Warrior wasn't even on the search committee that hired me. He was on leave that year. I didn't negotiate with him until months after I and UIUC signed the contract, when he resumed duties as unit director in summer 2014. My dealings were with Vince Diaz and Jodi Byrd, the committee chairs. I don't know why they selected me. I didn't attend their private deliberations. All I know is I submitted an application, went through a rigorous vetting process, and got offered a job, which I subsequently accepted. The cadre of sudden experts in all things Native knows even less. One problem with academics is that they think opinions are always welcome, particularly in moments when nobody requested them.

The timing of the firing left AIS in a bind. They needed to cover two courses that had already been enrolled. Everybody's workload increased. Management had formally ratified the unimportance of the department. All the ethnic studies units at UIUC were informed that, in the final balance, they simply don't matter.

The termination undermined a vision of AIS that entailed transnational ambitions. My hiring represented a formal conjoining of Palestine to Native North America and the Pacific. It would be a stretch to say that management intentionally sought to damage these relationships; I rather doubt it possesses either the knowledge or cleverness to carry out that deed. On the other hand, academic critique of colonization increasingly includes Zionism among its targets, so administrators have great impetus to forestall decolonial projects by protecting Israel from scrutiny, whose inevitable outcome is opprobrium. These rollbacks on all manner of decolonial scholarship are a common feature of the corporate university.

The University of Illinois administration maligned Native America and Palestine simultaneously. It did so by again conferring normativity to the commonsensical practices of US and Israeli imperialism. It requires a deeply civilized mind to accomplish all these things in so short a time without the faintest hint of self-awareness. Obliviousness, anyway, is how civility survives. The most consistent forms of violence in this world are the ones explained as natural human behavior. There is nothing more natural than our Godly responsibility to perpetually renew the purity of the American landscape.

TWELVE

Shame on Me

L ife has been chaotic since Wise's letter arrived on August 2, 2014.[31] Getting the letter on a Saturday was a curse. Diana and I had to wait nearly two days until anybody would be on campus. We forwarded the message to a lawyer who had advised us during the "support our troops" kerfuffle. He was on vacation in Italy, but, in an act of generosity I consider life-saving, sprung to action, giving us advice and contacting colleagues who might help. We worked closely until I ended up settling on my current legal team, which includes the Center for Constitutional Rights. The University of Illinois ruined not only my career but a brilliant lawyer's Italian vacation.

That Saturday, I spoke with Robert Warrior and Jodi Byrd, acting head of AIS when I was recruited and hired. They were equally stunned. Both expressed concern about my family's well-being. The entire department was supportive. No matter what happens, I will always be honored to call them my colleagues. Robert and Jodi both assured me that they would investigate the matter and still expected to welcome me to the department. There was nothing to do but wait.

---

31. Although the letter is dated August 1, 2014, Wise didn't email it to me until the next day, a Saturday. Or, it didn't arrive until Saturday. The timestamp on the email is August 2.

I kept the news quiet. I knew that media coverage would weaken the possibility of resolving the problem. I figured that if the story went public, people would invest themselves in various positions and make everything intractable. I was committed to working it out behind closed doors with university administrators. It turns out that I never had an opportunity to speak with Wise. Events in subsequent months showed that UIUC would have been unwilling to reconsider its decision.

I had to tell my parents, siblings, and in-laws, though. Doing so was probably the most difficult part of the ordeal. My parents were supportive, but visibly worried. I hated that they'd seen their three children become successful and self-sufficient only for one of them to lapse into dependence. I knew that they'd become even more worried once people began talking about me. My siblings, with whom I'm extremely close, responded in the best way possible, as did my in-laws, with whom I'm also extremely close. Nobody chided or upbraided me. They made arrangements to help.

But the feelings of shame didn't abate.[32] I couldn't face Diana. I felt like a failed father. I began smoking too many cigarettes. I ate unhealthy food at odd hours. I refused to sleep until after dropping off my son at school. In my mind, I had let down my family; nothing would move me from that perception. My default personality is happy, but stress can be a more forceful motivator. I recognized that I needed to restore myself to a more congenital disposition, but I had no energy for this sort of readjustment. It can be difficult to comprehend how important our careers are to our identities until we no longer have them.

Having been trained in so many environments to automatically side with sites of power, it's difficult for us to discern the inequitable dynamics of controversy, even when we exist as controversial subjects.

---

32. I really hope I'm not giving Orientalists fodder for some cultural analysis of shame in the Arab mind.

Immediately after I was fired, a small army of people began digging through every word I'd ever written and scouring my past (including family histories) to retroactively justify their support for UIUC's indefensible decision. (As a general rule, a decision can be seen as indefensible if its rationale demands the defamation of its victim.) Folks disparaged my academic writing, though UIUC management never claimed its action had anything to do with scholarship. They cited my online book reviews. They used iPhones to record my private conversations. Everything in my past was a public document. My flaws became a referendum on Israel's survival.

What had I done to those seeking to discredit and humiliate me? Why did it take me months to ask this simple question? Those conducting the witch hunt—itself a pretty damning indicator of dishonor—aligned with a force that had undermined my livelihood. In other words, I hadn't done shit to these people. But they have plenty of reason to explain their own behavior. Look no further if you want a good example of how normativity works.

Diana was more than supportive; she assumed every crucial household role and executed them with vigor. She is great in peaceful moments and even better in crisis. We work well together. She responded to my depression with both tough and tender emotion. She too had resigned from a good job at Virginia Tech. She began work at a clothing retailer in Northern Virginia, to which she commuted an hour each way. She would later accept a student affairs job at Georgetown University, which provided us health insurance after six months without coverage, a scary proposition for any family with a toddler. Being uninsured put into sharp relief something about which I always possessed too little awareness: the difficulties of an uninsured life. The unawareness arose from both personal failure and the professional cultures in which we often take privilege for granted.

On Tuesday, August 5, Scott Jaschik from *InsideHigherEd.com* began calling. He was on to the story. I don't know how he learned of it, but when I finally answered his call it was clear that his sense of the situation was accurate. Somebody had leaked information. Whoever did it was in the know. I told Jaschik that I wasn't able to comment and then braced myself.

Pandemonium followed the appearance of Jaschik's article the next morning. The phone didn't stop ringing. Friends were wondering what the hell had happened and media wanted me to say something. I was stunned by some of the requests: CNN, Al Jazeera, Fox News, the *Chicago Tribune*, CBS News, the *Chronicle of Higher Education*, the *Los Angeles Times*, the *Guardian*, the Associated Press. Every time I checked email there were dozens of new messages. My Twitter followers ballooned. I had become a virus on Facebook.

My lawyer insisted that I remain quiet, which wasn't difficult. I was too overwhelmed to have said anything remotely coherent. I knew the termination would generate interest, but I assumed it largely would be limited to local media, scholarly blogs, and academic trade publications. I had prepared myself for an outpouring of response from colleagues, not from corporate media.

The stress was compounded by the fact that Diana and I needed a place to live. We were to close on a condo in Savoy, just south of Champaign, the following week. The seller, a lawyer, was displeased, to put it mildly. We resigned ourselves to the fact that our earnest money wasn't coming back. (Neither was the deposit we had already given to our son's daycare, the one on UIUC's campus.) We couldn't stay in our Blacksburg home. We had already rented it to a tenant whose lease began a few days prior. His stuff filled our basement; he lived in a hotel while awaiting our departure.

Staying, then, wasn't an option. Even if we could have brought ourselves to remove our tenant's belongings and tell him to scram— not a chance—we had no way to pay our mortgage. For the first time since I was seventeen, I would have to live in the home of another family member. That home ended up being in the DC suburbs, where my parents own a townhouse. The problem then became how to get there. UIUC had already arranged movers to lug our belongings to Illinois. That option no longer existed. We'd have to move ourselves, with little preparation and a constricted timeline. Fitting the contents of a 2,700-square-foot house into a smaller townhouse already inhabited by people with their own belongings wouldn't be easy, so we began our move by donating or tossing a considerable portion of our possessions.

My two brothers-in-law came down to help. In a day, we boxed the entire house and loaded it onto a truck. Diana's brothers returned to their wives in the DC area. Diana, our son, and I slept in our house one last time, on a futon mattress on the floor, our voices echoing across empty rooms. The next day, we stuffed the mattress into the back of a packed U-Haul and drove to Northern Virginia, where we stacked boxes in my parents' one-car garage.

In the meantime, media coverage hadn't slowed. I was gagged. I would remain silent for more than a month, until giving a press conference in Urbana on September 9, two days before the board of trustees rejected my appointment. I received more messages than I could return. I encountered more ignorant things on the Internet than I care to confess having read. We learn in these situations how racist assumptions guide engagement with self-professed devotion to detached reason.

As we settled into our new place, I began to recover my sense of character. Beyond Diana's care and attention, I attribute the recovery to the intervention of both friends and strangers. I particularly remember chatting with Lisa Kahaleole Hall and J. Kehaulani Kauanui on the same day (in separate conversations)[33] and getting schooled on the abusive dynamics of colonial induction. I learned to ignore the noise of the story.

---

33. It's true: I actually answered the phone twice on the same day. I can't imagine it ever happening again.

The press conference was a moment of tremendous pride. My lawyers devised the idea of releasing my first public statement in Champaign-Urbana. We knew that if the event were held on campus the administration would view it as hostile, so, working with some UIUC faculty, we booked the Urbana YMCA, a wonderful old building that proved perfect for the occasion. The legal team suspected that there would be enough media interest to justify the decision. They were correct.

Diana and I rode to Urbana from Chicago with Matthew Shenoda, with whom we had stayed. Two hours of Matthew's calm intellect with a backdrop of Bob Marley was a terrific way to travel. Matthew is a practicing Copt; his place is filled with intricate symbols of his faith. As we were leaving his apartment, I asked him if he had an icon I could carry in my pocket. As he rummaged, his four-year-old daughter brought me a photo of my namesake, Saint Stephen, Christianity's protomartyr. He was stoned to death for passionately denouncing authority.

I have little idea why I was compelled in that moment to ask for a religious icon. The moment seemed to demand it. I wanted to carry on my body a physical simulation of my ancestors. I put the laminated icon inside my left breast pocket. I remembered it when I walked to the microphone. I tapped at it with my right hand in appreciation, and in recognition of the audience, when I had finished speaking.

Two of my lawyers, Anand Swaminathan of Loevy and Loevy and Maria LaHood of the Center for Constitutional Rights, rode together from Chicago. We met at Urbana's Caffe Paradiso in the morning. I realized how much coverage my firing had generated locally when some of the patrons pointed at me and whispered. Anand and Maria provided last-minute coaching: keep collected, answer with confidence, be true to your personality, respond to hostile questions with an even tone, stick to a narrow set of imperatives, provide your own answers to off-topic inquiries.[34]

Once the coaching ended, I ordered a double espresso and stepped outside for a smoke. I don't get nervous speaking publicly. This time I was nervous. The cigarette shook in my fingers. I would have eagerly traded nicotine for tetrahydrocannabinol in that moment.

An hour later, we were ushered into the YMCA auditorium through the kitchen of a Chinese restaurant housed in the building. I was stunned when we entered the auditorium from a side door leading to the dais. A huge crowd stood and chanted "Reinstate Salaita." The space was packed to capacity. Many others stood outside of the auditorium in the foyer. Dozens of reporters occupied the front few rows. Lights flashed from expensive cameras perched atop tripods. I knew in that moment we would win this battle. I smiled and waved. I was drenched from the steady rain on the four-block walk from the car to the building. In pictures, I look afflicted by irregular splotches of sweat.

I had the opportunity to hear Eman Ghanayem and Rico Kleinstein Chenyek, AIS graduate students, deliver a fabulous speech in tandem about the systemic marginalization of Palestine, and endemic racism more broadly, on campus. Michael Rothberg, chair of English and director of the Initiative in Holocaust, Genocide, and Memory Studies, read a statement condemning the university's action from the Modern Language Association. Robert Warrior spoke expansively and brilliantly about what it means to be an engaged intellectual in the neoliberal university. Maria began things with a take-no-prisoners denunciation of Israeli brutality and the legal problems of punishing those who condemn it.

The best part of the day was getting to chat, however briefly, with the folks at UIUC who had become like family to me. (I

---

34. There's something unnerving about a lawyer with no personal commitment to justice; there is much admirable about one who views justice as something more than a professional obligation.

quickly realized that certain members of the media are adept at sneaking around private conversations with tape recorders.)

The students and faculty of UIUC became my salvation after the firing. On that day in Urbana, I grabbed tightly to the lifeline they had offered me.

There was no longer any doubt: I would fight. And, just like the Palestinians on whose behalf so many of us work, I have no intention of stopping.

THIRTEEN

The Evolution of "Anti-Semitism"

Being called anti-Semitic isn't as trenchant as it used to be. When we hear the accusation, Israeli policy and the discourses used to justify it usually become relevant. We must then parse how a nation-state can or should act as an emissary of a cultural or ethnic community. I contend that nation-states, which necessarily practice violence, can never embody the values of their citizens, if only because minority groups are inevitably excluded from primary national identities.

I want to make something clear: I hate anti-Semitism. "Hate" is a strong word, which is precisely why I use it. As I've said many times before, I would like to share both a nation and a national identity with my Jewish brothers and sisters. No Zionist I know shares that sentiment.

Yet my tweets have been called anti-Semitic. It is apparently one of the reasons for which I was fired. The claims of anti-Semitism are feeble and deceitful. Of the tweets cited as "intemperate" or "angry" by those justifying my termination, none deals with anything other than Israel. It's clear, then, that tone and language aren't actually the problem. According to the commonplaces of respectable political thought, criticism of Israel is necessarily intemperate no matter the tone and language by which it is conducted.

Nor have critics cited my many tweets condemning anti-Semitism or proclaiming that Arabs and Jews are brethren and should therefore be treated equally. The tweets that critics ignore are more important to understanding my firing than the tweets they cite. My denunciations of Israel and Zionism aren't as threatening as my calm appeals to humanism. The idea of equality becomes "anti-Semitic" merely by its unwillingness to submit to the demands of ethnocracy. I didn't articulate anti-Semitism. I disparaged Judeo-supremacy.

Few have noted that my Twitter comments are derivative of longstanding Jewish intellectual traditions. Indeed, part of the comments' rationale is to convey some of the central tenets of those traditions and thus illustrate that Zionism has never existed in lockstep with Jewish thought (and certainly not as the singular emissary of Jewish identity). The relationship, in fact, has been richly debated and at times deeply tense.

Thinkers who have explored these questions include both liberals and leftists, some of whom predate Israel's founding: Hannah Arendt, Michael Lerner, Noam Chomsky, Ahad Ha'am, Martin Buber, Ella Habiba Shohat, Norman Finkelstein, Albert Einstein, Tony Judt, and Joel Kovel. It is a distinguished list.

Let's take, for example, Michael Neumann, who once observed,

It gets worse if anti-Zionism is labeled antisemitic, because the settlements, even if they do not represent fundamental aspirations of the Jewish people, are an entirely plausible extension of Zionism. To oppose them is indeed to be anti-Zionist, and therefore, by the stretched definition, antisemitic. The more antisemitism expands to include opposition to Israeli policies, the better it looks. Given the crimes to be laid at the feet of Zionism, there is another simple syllogism: anti-Zionism is a moral obligation, so, if anti-Zionism is antisemitism, antisemitism is a moral obligation.

Judith Butler puts it this way:

It is untrue, absurd, and painful for anyone to argue that those who formulate a criticism of the State of Israel is anti-Semitic or, if Jewish, self-hating. Such charges seek to demonize the person who is articulating a critical point of view and so disqualify the viewpoint in advance. It is a silencing tactic: this person is unspeakable, and whatever they speak is to be dismissed in advance or twisted in such a way that it negates the validity of the act of speech. The charge refuses to consider the view, debate its validity, consider its forms of evidence, and derive a sound conclusion on the basis of listening to reason. The charge is not only an attack on persons who hold views that some find objectionable, but it is an attack on reasonable exchange, on the very possibility of listening and speaking in a context where one might actually consider what another has to say.

It is not only thinkers on the left who complicate tidy conflations of anti-Semitism with criticism of Israel. There is a long history of it among Orthodox Jews and ultranationalist Zionists. Although I dislike his moral point of view, Likud godfather Ze'ev (Vladimir) Jabotinsky was one of the most sober and compelling analysts of Jewish identity and ethnonationalism. I have said nothing that Jabotinsky didn't say first. The main difference is that Jabotinsky endorsed a sort of realism I consider unjust and untenable.

Here is one of his most notable formulations:

Those who hold that an agreement with the natives is an essential condition for Zionism can now say "no" and depart from Zionism. Zionist colonization, even the most restricted, must either be terminated or carried out in defiance of the will of the native population. This colonization can, therefore, continue and develop only under the protection of a force independent of the local population—an iron wall which the native population cannot break through. This is, in toto, our policy towards the Arabs. To formulate it any other way would only be hypocrisy.

Jabotinsky makes a straightforward point, one that I merely repeat, about the incompatibility of ethnocracy and democracy. To consider them compatible is a liberal Zionist conceit, one whose inconceivability has been critiqued since well before 1948. There is nothing anti-Semitic about suggesting that liberal Zionists need to take ownership of the violence required to uphold a system in which one group of people is afforded rights denied to another group based on nothing more than state-sanctioned religious identity. The imperative is simple: you can either have a "Jewish" state or you can have a legitimate democracy, but you cannot have both.

No less a Zionist than Meir Kahane[35] once said,

> Let me explain why everybody is mad at me. It's because I have confronted people with the following contradiction: you can't have Zionism and democracy at the same time. And for those who criticize me, it's very difficult to get out of this contradiction. [. . .] First of all, Western democracy has to be ruled out. For me that's cut and dried: there's no question of setting up democracy in Israel, because democracy means equal rights for all, irrespective of racial or religious origins. Therefore democracy and Zionism cannot go together. And Israel's Declaration of Independence, which proclaimed this state to be a Jewish state, is a totally schizophrenic document. You just can't, on the one hand, want a Jewish state and at the same time give non-Jews the right to become a majority. When Abba Eban makes beautiful speeches in twelve languages and starts talking about Jewish democracy—what on earth does that mean, Jewish democracy?

I agree with the principle Kahane puts forward, that there's no such thing as a real democracy based on conquest and demographic manipulation. I disagree with him that conquest and demographic ma-

---

35. Kahane founded the Jewish Defense League [JDL] in 1968 and served a term in the Knesset. He believed in the forced expulsion of all Arabs from Israel.

nipulation are desirable. I rarely see liberal Zionists offer the same moral distance on these two points.

As much as it pains me to admit it, I said nothing new on Twitter; I merely expressed ethical points of view about a debate that is at least a century old and shocking only to those who know little about the philosophical and political history of Zionism.

If I might add to this long intellectual tradition, let's consider a tweet I sent on July 19, 2014:

> At this point, if Netanyahu appeared on TV with a necklace made from the teeth of Palestinian children, would anybody be surprised? #Gaza

This observation led to accusations of anti-Semitism. I will address those accusations in a moment. First, some context. At that point Netanyahu's government had killed nearly three hundred children in Gaza. My post was a perfectly valid way to use hyperbole to highlight the barbarity of his deeds. The point is not complicated: Netanyahu was consciously killing children, so why should we be surprised if he looks as horrible as his actions suggested? Netanyahu, quite frankly, deserved stronger condemnation.

As to the notion that I invoked images of "blood libel": actually, no I did not; I invoked images of a murderous politician to suggest that apparently he can kill as many children as he likes without generating the ire of the American government. Those calling me anti-Semitic put the blood libel discourse into play. There is no tradition in the hideous annals of blood libel imagery of showing Jews wearing necklaces made of teeth. Arabs and Muslims too were victims of blood libel narratives in both pre- and post-industrial Europe. The image of Netanyahu wearing a necklace made of teeth more appropriately belongs to the category of satire in relation to allegories of political trophyism.

I criticized Netanyahu as a prime minister, not as a Jew. That so many felt compelled to conceptualize criticism of a head of state busy slaughtering children as an attack against a Jew validates concern about the dangers of conflating Israel with Jewishness. Let's go ahead and start calling denunciation of Harper, Obama, and Cameron anti-Christian. (Or anti-Muslim for Obama, so the Tea Party won't be confused.)

Why, anyway, must folks who have never uttered an anti-Semitic statement constantly make our opposition to anti-Semitism explicit? Nobody else has to proclaim opposition to things they've never endorsed as a precondition of speaking. More important, why don't those who repeatedly disparage Palestinians ever have to answer to their troublesome beliefs? I'd love to see folks who condone the slaughter of children and the illegal settlement of foreign territory disavow themselves of anti-Arab racism.

It's because Israel, like the whiteness it epitomizes, is the default norm of civility. Israelis are assumed to be human; to criticize them, then, is inherently aggressive. Palestinians, on the other hand, must loudly denounce aggression at every imaginable moment in order to be considered human in the first place, even as we suffer the unrelenting violence of Israeli colonization. Our barbarity is atavistic and immanent. It precedes our subjectivity, restricts our earthly presence, and marks us as inferior. We can achieve the lofty status of pitiable only when we grovel. We constitute a species that must genuflect in order to earn the trust of those by whom we are conquered and defined.

I am no anti-Semite. I say it clearly, and for the last time. I now await my detractors' proclamations that they consider Palestinians worthy of respect and equality.

FOURTEEN

Puffery

My experience of being smeared as anti-Semitic has been deeply unpleasant. It resulted from consummate disingenuity. Those who proffer such accusations should be responsible for providing the evidence, yet it is I, like all anti-Zionists who suffer the same slander, who has been saddled with the impossible task of disproving a negative.

To return to Kennedy's audacious quote: "We were sort of stunned that anyone would write such blatantly anti-Semitic remarks." UIUC faculty members Joyce Tolliver[36] and Nick Burbules, who are known around campus for sanctimonious devotion to administrative corruption, suggest, "The real issue is with the form and substance of Salaita's comments. He has made numerous public statements over the summer that are not just 'strident and vulgar,' but are, in the view of many people, incendiary and anti-Semitic."

The Kennedy quote is an example of his proclivity to feign gravitas where fatuity prevails. Many Jewish people associated with UIUC, including Michael Rothberg, pleaded with Kennedy to reconsider his characterizations of my tweets, but without success. Productive conversation about the uses of this terminology is possi-

---

36. You can find everything you need to know about Tolliver on her UIUC faculty page, where she is listed as "Dr. Joyce Tolliver PhD."

ble, and desirable, but Kennedy forestalled that possibility by insisting on the supremacy of his interpretation. Such insistence reveals the problems of top-down management in university settings. Experts on the campus Kennedy oversees, along with students, instructors, and community members who self-identify as Jewish, stated that I cannot be reasonably implicated as anti-Semitic, but Kennedy ignored their voices, choosing instead to entertain the outrage of donors and partisan activists. This sort of problem often affects the corporate university, as many upper administrators avoid community engagement in an effort to relentlessly appease the powerful.

The Tolliver and Burbules passage is more insidious. (I confess: "insidious" is but a civil way to say "fainthearted.") Perhaps cognizant of the possibility of libel, they attribute my anti-Semitism to unnamed observers. Theirs is a mealy-mouthed argument, proffering a remarkable claim while releasing themselves of consequence or responsibility. That argument doesn't represent a discourse; it is the archetype of elision, a pious device of sophistry and microaggression. Tolliver and Burbules offer an impeccable example of civilized defamation.

They are also less than forthcoming about their discussion with administrators in the days leading to the termination. Emails produced through Freedom of Information Act (FOIA) requests show Burbules and Tolliver deliberating with Wise and Provost Ilesanmi Adesida about how to handle their "concerns." (In their exchanges Wise laments that my offending tweets were sent "after the decision to hire him.") In their op-ed, Burbules and Tolliver call for an "honest debate" without disclosing their apparent complicity with management. They remark, "Since neither the university nor Salaita has spoken publicly about the issue, there is much we do not know." I reckon an "honest debate" should probably include acknowledgment of what two of the participants in the decision did know but chose not to reveal.

Burbules and Tolliver's furtive collusion with management and their deceitful article provide terrific examples of how faculty can enact the dispossession of their colleagues, thus acting as functionaries of administrative interests. They reproduce the mental habits of colonial induction and tacitly demand adherence to the archetypes of managerial pragmatism, doing so both publicly and anonymously. I cannot determine which is worse: working in anonymity on behalf of administrative (read: corporate) interests or attaching one's name to it. Whatever the case, one thing is certain: Burbules and Tolliver are stupid for doing the work of an upper administrator at the salary of a professor.

Staying in the realm of faculty who supplement administrative interests, nobody has supported UIUC more doggedly than erstwhile UIUC professor Cary Nelson, the former AAUP president and theorist of academic freedom who, in the grand tradition of know-nothing Orientalists, has become the go-to commentator on everything from Palestinian culture to Indigenous Studies. It's useful to assess the rationale for his support of the UIUC administration as an exercise in identifying the dramaturgy necessary for self-styled progressives to accept Zionism. Nelson exemplifies the inconsistencies that arise when emotional attachment to Israel encounters anti-Zionist critique. Assessing a few of his statements illuminates those inconsistencies:

- "Although I was not involved in the process [of Salaita's hiring] and did not communicate my views to the administration, I want to say why I believe the decision not to offer him a job was the right one."
- "Faculty members are well within their rights to evaluate someone as a potential colleague and to consider what contributions a candidate might make to the campus community."
- "I should add that this is not an issue of academic freedom.

If Salaita were a faculty member here and he were being sanctioned for his public statements, it would be."

- "It is the whole Salaita package that defines in the end the desirability and appropriateness of offering him a faculty appointment."
- "I believe this was an academic, not a political, decision."
- "His tweets are the sordid underbelly, the more frank and revealing counterpart, to his more extended arguments about Middle Eastern history and the Israeli/Palestinian conflict. They are likely to shape his role on campus when 2015's Israeli Apartheid Week rolls around. I am told he can be quite charismatic in person, so he may deploy his tweeting rhetoric at public events on campus."
- "Academic freedom protects [Salaita] from university reprisals for his extramural speech."
- "I regret that the [university's] decision was not made until the summer, but then many of the most disturbing of Salaita's tweets did not go online until the summer of 2014, no doubt provoked by events. That is the time frame in which the statements in question were made. That alone made this an exceptional case. I do not think it would have been responsible for the university to have ignored the evolving character of his public profile."

All of these passages are from *the same* essay. As a service to the reader, allow me to translate the argument:

Salaita's firing was not political. I repeat, *not* political. I rerepeat, NOT political. Nor is it an issue of academic freedom. It has *nothing to do with academic freedom*, because if it does then I can't reconcile my reputation as czar of the phenomenon and still own my role in the firing of a tenured professor for acts of extramural speech. It's a contractual issue. What's that? Salaita signed a contract, as did the university? Whoops, never mind. It's all about his horrible tweets and all the mean things he might say while on campus, but, remember, it's not political. I detest his criticism of Israel, but, reremember, it's *not* political. Salaita's tweets were provoked by events in Israel and Gaza, but, rereremember, it's NOT political. I don't do political things. White males like Cary Nelson are capable of objectivity, see. We're never motivated by lower-order impulses of emotion and irrationality. These brown people can be very persuasive, you know. Charismatic, even. Students, in their bollixed naiveté, might not be able to distinguish between a responsible, apolitical educator like Cary Nelson and a babbling savage like Steven Salaita. That's why Palestinians must always raise their arguments through the mediated altruism of judicious supporters of military occupation, because we have no vested interest in Israel. Oh, and this whole donor thing? I have no idea what you're talking about.

Nelson exemplifies the rhetorical incoherence of UIUC's supporters. The evidence of Zionist malfeasance in academe is everywhere. When the movement for a boycott of Israeli universities delivered fantastic results last year, self-righteous Zionists opposed it on the grounds of academic freedom. (They fooled nobody.) We stated repeatedly that one of the goals of BDS is to protect the rights of those who dare criticize Israel. Few things are easier than being proved correct by overzealous Zionists, what with their visceral reliance on the force of institutions to instill discipline among the resistant.

The rhetorical incoherence I cite is evident in the ever-evolving justifications for my firing, a pattern that emerges whenever a critic of Israel comes under attack. First I was anti-Semitic. Then I was uncivil. Then I was a bad teacher. Then I was too charismatic. Then I was too angry. Then I was too profane. Then I was too radical. Then I was too unpatriotic. Then I wasn't really hired. Then I was unqualified in the field of American Indian Studies. Then I benefitted from nepotism. Then I was a poor scholar. Then my colleagues were incompetent. Then my colleagues were deceitful. Then my colleagues were ignorant. Then the American Indian Studies Program required special guidance. Then the decision to hire me was solely based on politics. Then Indigenous Studies was illegitimate. Then the entire damn field needed to be shut down.

Despite the jumbled rhetoric, there exists a persistent consistency in the inconsistent rationales in support of UIUC: condemnation of Zionism must be punished. And those who deliver the punishment must never admit that their real motivation is to discipline scholars who don't kowtow to colonial power. The person who adheres to a politics he refuses to claim surely occupies a profoundly sad existence.

I would reprimand these pitiful dissemblers for casting stones, but we know they're way too afraid of Palestinian agency to appreciate the metaphor.

≈

I'm not done with the matter of anti-Semitism. The term and its practice implicate Jewish people, but when Zionists deploy it to discourage criticism of Israel it summons a set of racialized discourses. It thus intersects, and participates in, the practices of American racism. I have spent much time exploring the dangers of conflating Jewish peoplehood with the practices of a nation-state and the apocryphal notions of anti-Semitism that emerge from that conflation; I want to now situate these apocryphal notions of anti-Semitism into frameworks of normative whiteness.

Upon any accusation of anti-Semitism, it is the responsibility of the accuser to supply evidence for his or her claim. The accusation delegitimizes anybody who has criticized Israel and thus renders itself less a strategy of identifying racism than of exercising it through furtive reproductions of majoritarian angst. That angst is connected to the commonplaces of reverse racism and white retrenchment.[37] The normal convention of supplying evidence dissipates, replaced by a need for the accused to reaffirm her humanity in the face of an association with Palestinians. The charge of anti-Semitism, when directed against the anti-Zionist, presupposes fundamentally racist attitudes toward Arabs and Muslims.

The history of anti-Semitism, along with its practice, is long and complex, as are its many uses in imaginaries of the Jew. I do not purport to examine anti-Semitism in its totality, if such a move is even possible. Instead, I limit myself to its use as a rhetorical device and as a form of moralistic persuasion in discourses of Zionist exceptionalism. I needn't be Jewish or a historian of anti-Jewish racism to claim authority on the subject. As somebody of (partial) Palestinian origin, deeply concerned with the colonization of my ancestral land, I consider it necessary to identify and assess how Zionists rationalize the Israeli colonial project. A key element of this rationalization is the evolution of the term "anti-Semitism" and the new meanings it acquires in relation to Israeli violence.

There is much chatter about how anti-Semites find cover in anti-Israel rhetoric. Writing in the *Guardian*, Emanuele Ottolenghi claims, "Despite piqued disclaimers, some of Israel's critics use anti-semitic stereotypes. In fact, their disclaimers frequently offer a mask of respectability to otherwise socially unacceptable anti-semitism." Steven Bayne offers a similar analysis: "A respectable anti-Zionism theoretically may well exist. But in the context of the twenty-first century, with Israel increasingly the hub of Jewish life and facing daily assaults upon her very existence, those who embrace anti-Zionism need to acknowledge that they allow no room for Jewish self-determination and reject the right of the Jews to sustain their distinct and meaningful sense of peoplehood."

---

37. "White retrenchment" refers to an increased investment in whiteness as a source of authentic national identity.

It is true that anti-Semitism can be articulated through a prism of anti-Zionism. Notable purveyors of this strategy include David Duke and Pat Buchanan. There have been moments when individuals posted an anti-Semitic trope or formulation in the various spaces of Palestine solidarity. However, the Palestine solidarity community in both the Arab World and North America has been vigilant in making clear that its problem begins and ends with Zionist colonization. Nor can proponents of the view that anti-Zionists often articulate anti-Semitism find convincing examples of a prominent Palestine solidarity activist or scholar disparaging the Jewish people or religion. Ali Abunimah, As'ad AbuKhalil, Rasmea Odeh, Magid Shihade, Noura Erekat, Joseph Massad, Rania Khalek, Sunaina Maira, David Lloyd, Bill Mullen, Dunya Alwan, Nada Elia, Remi Kanazi, Rima Najjar, Nadine Naber, Lara Deeb—each person, without fail, diligently castigates anti-Semites of all varieties. It is a crucial feature of Palestine solidarity activism to eradicate the existence of anti-Semitism throughout the world.

Those affiliated with BDS, along with the movement itself, often field accusations of anti-Semitism. For example, in a 2014 speech Binyamin Netanyahu proclaimed, "The founders of the BDS movement make their goals perfectly clear. They want to see the end of the Jewish state. They're quite explicit about it. And I think it's important that the boycotters must be exposed for what they are. They're classical anti-Semites in modern garb." Though it should require no clarification, Netanyahu's claim is nonsensical, one neither he nor anybody else can substantiate.[38] In fact, nobody has found evidence of this anti-Semitism among members of the USACBI Organizing Collective, a multiethnic and multidenominational group. One can certainly find principled statements of opposition to Zionism, some

---

38. Leave it to Netanyahu to imply that wearing trousers constitutes an act of anti-Semitism.

of them passionate, but nothing that disparages Jews or Judaism.[39]

Given everything that the people of Palestine have lost and suffered, and the constant insistence among Zionists that Israel embodies Jewish culture, it's actually quite remarkable that Palestinians take such care to distinguish the Israeli state from those it purports to represent. It is likewise remarkable that most Palestinians of the West Bank and Gaza consistently say they're willing to share the land with Israeli Jews.[40]

Palestine solidarity activists too have struggled in the service of ethical practices. Despite not always succeeding, we work hard to maintain the distinction between Jewish peoplehood and the state of Israel, in contradistinction to the Zionists who insist the two are indivisible. According to Robert Fulford, "It's now almost automatic for liberals and socialists to see Israel as a colonial power imposed on a comparatively helpless people. And dislike of Israel easily turns into dislike of diaspora Jews who support Israel." Bernard-Henri Lévy points to three factors that motivate anti-Semitism vis-à-vis Israel:

1.   Jews are detestable because they are inseparable from a detestable state. This is the anti-Zionist tenet.

2.   Jews are all the more detestable because the cement that holds that state together is the belief in a persecution that may well be imaginary or, at the very least, exaggerated. This is the negationist tenet, the tenet of Holocaust denial.

3.   By operating thus and cornering the market on the world's

---

39. In any case, I don't know that disparaging Judaism is automatically anti-Semitic, just as I am skeptical that disparaging Islam is Islamophobic or that disparaging Christianity is bigoted. The fact remains, though, that USACBI Organizing Collective members have refrained from such disparagement.

40. Polls purporting to gauge Palestinian attitudes show wildly differing results, but numerous recent surveys indicate that most Palestinians now reject a two-state solution and prefer binationalism; they likewise eschew violence as a means to achieve that outcome.

available reserves of compassion, the Jews heap on top of that twin injury the insult of rendering humanity deaf to the sufferings of other peoples, beginning, of course, with the Palestinians. This is the tenet of competitive victimhood.

If we accept as a general, if crude, proposition that anti-Semitism is the dislike of Jews, or those perceived to be Jews, based on culture, genetics, religious practice, theology, dress, appearance, or attitude, or the attribution of essences to a group of people imagined to be genetically predisposed to unsavory inborn characteristics, then Fulford and Lévy come dangerously close to rationalizing or rehearsing the phenomenon. Fulford totalizes Diaspora Jews as supporters of Israel and then attaches their likability—even their identity—to the behavior of Israel. Nobody is likeable in that circumstance.

Lévy's argument is the greater distortion. His first point posits that anti-Zionists consider Jews detestable because they view Jews as inseparable from a detestable state. Yet the vast majority of Israel's critics reject the conflation Lévy attributes to them; this rejection is the basis of anti-Zionist thought and theory. Lévy does precisely what he ascribes to the subjects of his criticism. His argument relies on the assumption that Israel never does wrong. In fact, Israel can do no wrong because it is a byproduct of an inviolate culture that transcends the normal impurities of political violence. Lévy manages to express anti-Semitism and philo-Semitism in the same paragraph.

Lévy deplores the mere existence of Palestinians. They interfered with an exceptional project. The Jews would have maintained their historical innocence had it not been for the inconvenience of Palestinian suffering, which is not worth empathy, but condemnation: the Palestinians represent a corrupting influence on a heretofore uncorrupted people. Lévy provides a terrific example of how the entrapments of race in age-old colonial mentalities can motivate the synthesis of anti-Zionism and anti-Semitism.

It doesn't make practical sense for Palestinians to promote the sort of conflation evident among Zionists, which perhaps informs their reluctance. Arabs and Muslims, on the whole, are skeptical of formulations that totalize communities or that associate citizens with governmental actions. Individuals who identify with these communities are accustomed to being blamed for transgressions that have nothing to do with them and thus being made, if only tacitly, to apologize for supposedly universal cultural failings. In societies beset by racist dynamics, the minority embodies the representational burden of an entire community, a burden many Zionists attempt to impose upon all Jews by conceptualizing Israel as an atavistic duty.

The problems of totalization don't merely extend to perception. Imperial practices require collective punishment, something Israel frequently does in the West Bank and Gaza (and against its own Palestinian citizens). Collective punishment of some variety is a hallmark of American policy in Iraq, Cuba, Iran, Afghanistan, North Korea, and Yemen. In turn, Arab and Muslim organizing generally avoids the pratfalls of essentialism, an avoidance common to all people of color in the United States. Because of these factors, along with a commitment to democratic national principles, it is easy for BDS thinkers and activists to separate Jewishness from Zionism. In this task, Zionist thinkers and activists haven't been nearly as successful.

FIFTEEN

The Lovely, Timeless Noise of Innocence

In Blacksburg, Virginia, the weather can be glorious in May. Evening thunderstorms are frequent, but the period is usually free of frost and offers warmth without humidity. The crisp smell of late May evokes months of relative peace, with students gone for the summer and the languid pace of Appalachia reasserting itself. I will always remember the season for the time I spent with our son on separate weeks exactly a year apart while Diana attended her professional conference.

Without her at home, I didn't trust myself to respond quickly to his cries if he awoke at night, so I slept on a folded Ikea futon next to his crib. During the day, I would load him into his stroller—the weight of twelve months entering my calves and triceps in the second summer—and walk around town, running errands and sitting on park benches, delighted by the surfeit of birds and squirrels and, in lucky moments, deer. I fed him pasta and ice cream and bathed him in honey-scented bubbles. After reading a small stack of books, I carried him to his crib and sat on the futon until he settled into sleep. A few hours later, after having relaxed in the living room,

I would tiptoe into the nursery and unwind, my feet inches from his head.

After we had to leave Blacksburg, I couldn't sleep. I ached for the comfort of that futon, slumbering in perfect temperament without a blanket or sheet, my son's heavy breathing interrupting ugly thoughts with the lovely, timeless noise of innocence.

SIXTEEN

The Chief Features
of Civility

Here is what civility looks like at the University of Illinois:

The above image derives from the erstwhile Chief Illiniwek, the official university mascot who was forcibly "retired" in 2007 because of the threat of NCAA sanction.

Lots of folks in Illinois are deeply attached to the chief. Or, as luck might have it, the chief is attached to them.

The chief, despite his ostensible retirement, is central to notions of civility and practices of diversity at UIUC. He is also partly responsible for my termination.

I can claim no special victimization by the chief, though. That ugly distinction belongs to my colleagues in American Indian Studies, who have suffered not only the indignities of the immortal mascot but an onslaught of racism from his obsessive supporters.

First things first: the chief is hideous. He represents no actual tribe, though his fans claim he is authentic.[41] His slogan is "Oskee Wow-Wow," which derives from the Native American language of Tontoese. He wears what appears to be the flag of Costa Rica on his cheeks. He is always solemn, even as he dances in buckskin and bare feet. He is meant to honor Natives, but in reality his function is to reaffirm the emotional desires of whiteness.

The chief is a psychic emblem of European settlement. There's a Facebook page devoted to him, with more than 62,000 members. The page is a testament to nostalgia, jingoism, angst, outrage, and indignation. Its users derive self-esteem from the animate implements of white supremacy. Take a look at some of the comments from a single thread, in response to the chief's surprise appearance at a football game:

- The French called them "Illiwek" as a show of respect. It meant "superior men." Why can't our generation continue to do the same???!!!

---

41. This is a tired form of colonial discourse: define "authentic" according to your own desires and then invoke authenticity when convenient. Native peoples themselves can never arbitrate the process, of course.

- Respect the Chief! Good things happen when he's there.
- It's amazing what the chief can do for our spirit
- I'm glad that The Chief made an appearance. What makes me sad is the fact that in these pictures, there is only 1 person, a little girl, who is doing what one should do when The Chief is present: arms held in front, folded over each other.
- See what happens when the Chief shows up...... Our spirit is renewed and we WIN! All hail the CHIEF!
- I saw him and it made me tear up a bit.
- Only reason they won, the warrior spirit was in the house!!!
- Okay Mom and Dad here is the chief!!! I know you would be watching. Mom and Dad went to the U of I and always loved the way the chief would do his dance. They would just like it greatly. I never heard my parents get so upset about something when the chief could no longer do his dance. I thought the [*sic*] only got upset with me. But that issue of the chief being put aside was a hard thing for them. They stopped any kind of support then to the U of I. All over this. Way to go Mom and Dad. I always love the way you would let your yes be yes and no be no. No sitting on the fence. Now I know where I get that.
- Chief = Win. Always has. Always will. Unfair play by the NCAA (rhymes for a reason)

I say this without snark or sarcasm: these folks don't need an Indian mascot; they need lots and lots of grief counseling.

Many a white person invested in the chief, or any other Indian mascot, claims an Irish ancestry flush with the horror of indentured servitude before announcing that he has no problem with Notre Dame's mascot. He just adores the leprechaun, in fact. This narrative doesn't quite constitute an argument; it is an assertion of primal belonging and its consequent privilege of naming the conditions of dishonor and complaint.

Notre Dame is an exception, however. It is the only high-profile Irish-themed mascot in the country. Compare the leprechaun with the hundreds, perhaps thousands, of Indian-themed teams at the high school, college, and professional levels. They are no aberration, but a phenomenon. It simply won't do to compare the Fighting Irish to the Fighting Illini. The latter doesn't stand alone like the former; it informs a longstanding process of appropriation in order to create simulations of white belonging. Those simulations often treat majoritarian angst as something sacred.

Such abundance of Native likenesses is no accident. Nearly absent from debate about mascots is the fact that Indian nations were colonized by the United States, leading not only to relationships of disparate power, but also to the fascination with the natives common to all colonial projects and the desire of the colonizer to maintain control of the historical and contemporary narratives of their encounter.

Indian mascots aren't fun-loving objects of admiration or a mere articulation of innocent fandom. Nor are they a legitimate attempt to "honor" Natives (a deed best accomplished, in any case, by listening to them rather than informing them what type of altruism they should accept—or, better yet, by supporting the implementation of treaty rights). Fans can absolutely root for Indian mascots without malice, but there is no escaping the fact that on a broader level those mascots are remnants of a colonial need to name, govern, and define. It is unhelpful to reduce the issue to individual intent when the problem is institutional.

If we are fully to make sense of the chief, then, we need to remove the conversation from conventional sites of multicultural politics and situate it in analysis of colonialism and its enduring legacies.

The Minnesota Vikings and Michigan State Spartans provide interesting corollaries to the chief; both evoke mythical symbols of the past. The peculiar iconography of the Indian mascot exists in this framework: an invention of the colonial gaze that signifies a sort of fierceness and nobility in an era of effete conciliation to politically correct forces. Of course, unlike Vikings and Spartans, Natives exist in the present, which is precisely why mascotry fails to justify its existence. If Indians had been fully exterminated, as many seem to believe has happened, then it might make sense to summon a romantic past as a self-referential sporting identity. As it happens, Natives are around to tell us what they think of the chief. They dislike him.

But Indian responses don't matter, unless they validate a colonial viewpoint, in which case they assume impervious authority. Mascotry is an issue of the settler's psychology. Natives play the role of antagonist in a majoritarian psychodrama. The chief has little to do with actual Indians and almost everything to do with the peculiar disquiet of a whiteness perceived to be in decline.

Whiteness has always been (partly) defined in contradistinction to the invented authenticity of the Indian, who is typecast as barbaric but romanticized as the shamanistic guide to North America's indigenous spaces, those mystical geographies of the settler's overactive imagination. (We see the same phenomenon in the Zionist appropriation of ostensibly Oriental culture, as when Israel Day celebrations feature traditional Arabic food, hookahs, and live camels.) The historical Indian, then, was dispossessed and has been retrofitted to Hollywood specifications, repatriated only to the extent that he can serve as a passive emblem of American identity.

Humane assimilationists of the past set out to save the man but kill the Indian. These days the goal is to save the fake Indian so we don't kill the white man.

The folks of the American Indian Studies Program at UIUC have spent considerable energy attempting to purge the chief from campus, to no avail. University leaders kowtow to influential alumni, who almost uniformly venerate the mascot. It represents the sum of their education, after all.

The chief isn't quite dead, even in official university sanction. In 2011, a disgruntled alumnus submitted a FOIA request after hearing rumors that the "Three in One," Indian-themed music that accompanied the chief's dances, might be scuttled. The request turned up email correspondence between Robert Warrior and then-interim chancellor Robert Easter.[42] Warrior explained to Easter, "By continuing the performance of this music after the retirement of the University's former sports mascot . . . campus leadership is promoting and tolerating a divisive and hostile campus climate for American Indian students, staff and faculty. Every time the band plays that music you are highlighting the institution's ugly past and pushing the campus backwards."

Media that reported Warrior's complaint largely missed the point. Warrior wasn't merely attempting to abolish idiotic music. He proffered a critique of campus climate from the point of view of Native peoples. While the alumnus who filed the FOIA request expressed a desire to retain the "Three in One," he appeared oblivious to broader issues of racism and hostility. The appeal to retaining the music was literal, while Warrior's assessment functioned at the level of symbolism—that is to say, Warrior recognized the imagery as symbolic of something other than the nostalgia of perturbed alumni, which is essentially a semiotics of selfishness.

There's an interesting dynamic at play in this situation, as in others regarding Indian mascotry. The chief, whatever else he may be considered, is first and foremost a brand. The deep attachment to him intimates an emotional and psychological investment in consumer culture. The university has a tremendous interest in maintaining that investment—it produces loyalty, which in turn produces the sort

---

42. Contrast the release of this correspondence with UIUC's reluctance to share documents pertaining to my firing.

of nostalgia that generates attachment and its desirable byproduct, alumni giving. The chief is a merchandised identity.

The chief is the most visible symbol of colonization and racism on campus, but those problems don't end with him. Under Chancellor Wise's watch, UIUC has suffered unacceptable institutional racism. In the late sixties, university leadership initiated the "Project 500," a campaign to boost Black enrollment to an almost-moderately tolerable level. In 1968, UIUC proudly enrolled 565 new Latinos and African Americans. By 2014, African American enrollment had changed dramatically. One might expect that after forty-six years, UIUC could finally crack quadruple digits. Not quite. In 2014, Black enrollment in the freshman class actually dropped 42 percent, to 356, the nadir (thus far) of a six-year decline. Wise arrived at UIUC in 2011.

This decline speaks to a pattern of minority (and working-class) enrollments across the United States. Remarkably, UIUC is in the top half of the Big Ten in percentage of Black students, at anywhere from 4.9 to 5.5 percent, depending on the source. The University of Minnesota tops out at 3.9 percent, while the University of Wisconsin-Madison, whose denizens brag endlessly about its diversity and lack of racism, boasts a robust 2.2 percent. At UCLA, a world-class public research institution located in a majority nonwhite city, African Americans comprise 3.9 percent of all students. A viral video from 2013 noted that among 2,418 new male students that fall, forty-eight were Black (no, I haven't omitted any zeroes). Across the country, the number of Black students has increased slightly while their graduation rates have fallen, indicative of, among other things, troublesome campus climates and lack of institutional support. (Certainly the low number of Black professors has something to do with those troublesome climates.) Meanwhile, Native enrollments remain low and graduation rates are 39 percent, as compared to 60 percent for white students, a similar problem of hostility and lack of support. At UIUC, where the ostensibly retired chief remains ubiquitous, Native enrollment is less than one hundred (of more than 42,000 students), a figure the university doesn't even bother to list on its website.

Moribund Black enrollment isn't the only issue affecting UIUC. Department of Urban and Regional Planning professor Stacy Harwood has documented a surfeit of racial aggression and microaggression on campus. A study in which Harwood participated found that (to quote directly from its findings):

- Nearly one out of every three students of color reported having their contributions minimized in class, being made to feel inferior in the classroom, and not being taken seriously in classes because of race.

- Over one out of three students of color have experienced harassment (emotional, verbal, or physical) on campus because of race.

- Over half of students of color reported having stereotypes made about them in the classroom because of race.

- Sixty percent of students of color have experienced racism on campus.

- Almost 80 percent of students of color have felt that the campus is informally segregated based on race.[43]

Harwood provides examples of numerous indignities, including a professor repeatedly using "nigger" in class, one openly disparaging a Chinese student, and another using the shopworn Socratic method against a Chicana student, asking her to illuminate the entire Mexican diaspora.

Civility assumes connotations based on the shifting dynamics of convention. The ability to name convention—that is, the standards of acceptable conduct—ties directly to power and prestige, itself a dubious concept. Institutional racism, long evident at UIUC,

---

43. The entire study can be found at: "Incivility and the Censored Voice in the Classroom," IRPH blog, Illinois Program for Research in the Humanities, September 25, 2014, https://iprh.wordpress.com/2014/09/25/incivility-in-the-classroom.

hides in the conventions of campus respectability. The diplomatic language of the sensible administrator or responsible scholar entails the unnamed violence of bureaucracy and tradition. (Think about the troublesome appeals embedded in most arguments in favor of "tradition.") Strong condemnation of that violence is necessarily uncivil because the beneficiaries of violence reproduce the prudence of their own authority.

When Wise, for instance, says, "Tenure . . . brings with it a heavy responsibility to continue the traditions of scholarship and civility upon which our university is built," she implicitly endorses institutional violence. The notion of "responsibility" in this context reaffirms traditions of the university (which include housing discrimination and segregation) rather than critical thought or intellectual independence. The university, like all land-grant institutions, was built upon the stolen land of Indigenous peoples, a reality that makes Wise's invocation of "civility" incredibly thoughtless. The presence of the chief, then, is perfectly appropriate to this halcyon vision of a university so awesome that it transcends everything, even its own history.

For this reason, bureaucrats can conceive of a campaign called "Inclusive Illinois" amid institutional policies of exclusion. They remain unaware of the ridicule that rapidly transforms the phrase into a punch line; they seem not to care about their hypocrisy, which, really, is every manager's prerogative. They then repeat the platitude to anybody who will listen—and to those who won't—as if to justify their mendacity by robotically broadcasting a comically ineffectual slogan.

Stupidity can be amusing—until the moment that stupidity also becomes a form of violence.

SEVENTEEN

The Disappearance of Print

People always ask me how it feels to be at the center of a huge controversy. I don't really know how to respond. Everything feels the same, only now a few more people give a damn.

I cherish the opportunity to share my scholarship with more people than I would have accessed had I not been banished from UIUC. I'm the rare scholar with—momentarily, at least—an audience. On the other hand, I was fired.

Fame is both negligible and subjective. In a tiny corner of a very small space my name has become familiar. I've even been recognized by strangers a few times, on both coasts. I've given talks with folks standing ten-deep in the corridor. But I doubt I'll be sneaking into buildings through the service entrance any time soon.

Still, this miniscule version of fame has been transformative. My life has evolved from one of persistent ennui to the chaos of continuous transit. My current job is to give public lectures, something that requires travel, which would be more tolerable if I didn't so deeply miss my wife and child. I also feel less confident running errands in my pajamas. Sure, this might seem like a silly complaint, but please believe me, puttin' on airs (as we say in Appalachia) fully contravenes my attachment to disorder. Even minor fame, you see, forces one to give a fuck what other people think.

I came to this realization one evening in Northern Virginia. I was out with Diana, our son, and her parents. We crowded around an outdoor table, everybody but me enjoying cups of Pinkberry frozen yogurt. I had opted for a syrupy drink—it would be offensive to label this sort of concoction a "coffee"—from the Peet's across the way. (Life in the DC suburbs requires brand-naming, which is crucial to the branding of the region's self-esteem.)

While waiting for my caffeinated sugar, I had noticed a table stacked with magazines. One of them was the *Vanity Fair* style issue, double the size of a normal edition. I did what any red-blooded American would do in the presence of a magazine produced by and for his blue-blooded compatriots: I took it.

This act might be perceived as dubious, for I took something that didn't belong to me—not exclusively, anyway—without paying for it. I'm comforted by the fact that I've not seen evidence that any corporate coffee shop has closed because of the prohibitive cost of not replacing missing reading material.

My removal of the magazine, anyway, was for the noblest of reasons: because I knew Diana would be interested in seeing the issue. (I'll not waste space confessing to my own tawdry fascination with high-society gossip.) I grabbed my drink, scooped the magazine, and walked briskly toward my family.

Diana was indeed happy, but her mother recoiled in exaggerated horror. She is a remarkable woman, my mother-in-law, born to poverty in Valencia, Venezuela, and self-made as a successful journalist. Even in retirement, she retains a keen eye and a deeply analytic mind, which complements her no-nonsense manner of speaking. I love and respect her deeply. I have always referred to her as *mi suegra*.

"*Aye, yerno*," she proclaimed, "people know you now. What would they say if they saw you take a magazine? Can you imagine the headlines?"

Actually, I can:

- Anti-Semitic Professor Steals Millions Worth of Couture
- Salaita Eschews Starbucks for Peet's; Caffeine, or Anti-Semitism?
- Despair Sets In as Hardworking, God-Fearing Americans Deprived of James Walcott's Snark
- Salaita Proves Arabs Are Predisposed to Theft
- Double the Incivility: Salaita Goes on Fashion Rampage
- Salaita Proves His Anti-Semitism by Declining to Steal the *New Republic*
- Salaita Breaks Commandments Against Theft and Graven Images
- Salaita Sneaks *Vanity Fair*, Seeks to Become More Civil
- Salaita Brazenly Robs Locally Owned Business
- Critic of Israel Mimics West Bank Settler
- Not Just the Settlers: Salaita Also Wants High Culture to Go Missing
- Breaking: Salaita Hates Pinkberry; "Tastes Like Piss," Says Foul-Mouthed Former Professor
- Salaita Makes Like Red Man, Stealthily Snatches White People
- Terror Averted When Swarthy Mocha-with-Soy Devotee Chooses Periodical over Suicide Bomb

EIGHTEEN

Injustice:
A Bull(shit) Market

I never had much affinity for authority. It's easy to think that no-body does, but in fact plenty of folks possess, for whatever reason, deeply authoritarian tendencies or a tendency to court authority. I was a timid kid, reluctant to accept physical challenges. My peers would dive from tall tree branches into swimming holes or spray dirt with motorbikes, their undersized tires sliding and squealing, but I merely watched, in a bit of awe, afraid of self-destruction. I always selected "truth" over "dare."

When it came to troublemaking, though, I was peerless. I thought nothing of deviance, disruption, truancy, dereliction, or in-subordination. I spent considerable time in or out of suspension. I knew, as all kids know, that adults are full of shit. Unlike many kids, thoroughly socialized into obedience, I acted on this reality. Children need to develop a type of literacy that allows them to ar-ticulate their natural skepticism; instead, we teach them to suppress their instinctual dissidence so they will be prepared for the rigor and discipline of a capitalist marketplace.

I hated being told what to do, but my folks were no acolytes of mollycoddled American parenting. They wielded the immigrant's guiding hand (and by "guiding," I mean "heavy"). We considered Mom the laxer, more pliable parent, but she could discipline with force if necessary. Dad was stubborn and stern, a man of effusive love but with little tolerance for laziness or sass. In difficult moments, I sometimes yearn for the comfort their presence provided my younger self, however confusing or arbitrary it appeared at the time. A child needs to feel safe. My parents, whatever their other successes or failings, offered safety.

Mom was more tolerant of my deviance. Her approach was to recognize the structural circumstances of my educational failings. Dad, in contrast, was an old-fashioned taskmaster. I learned later in life that he had an intimate understanding of the conditions that inspired me to fail, but in his mind they were merely inconveniences to overcome through focus and hard work. But Horatio Alger I was not. Whenever I was suspended, Dad woke me early and presented me a list of chores so strenuous I would be sore in the evening. It never worked. I would have rather mowed the lawn down to dirt than spend any time in school.

Those structural circumstances were universal to childhood instinct, but also specific to the environment in which I was raised. First of all, the education, strictly speaking, was terrible. In Bluefield, Virginia, we received luminous instruction in racial violence, verbal abuse, athletic douchebaggery, reckless testosterone, rape culture, androcentric nepotism, religious extremism, compulsory patriotism, relationships of disparate power, and pedagogical incompetence. Call it sociocultural schooling. It wasn't so useful in terms of intellectual development. We enjoyed third-rate facilities, unqualified teachers (in both approach and knowledge), outdated textbooks, dogmatic curricula, and a draconian environment.

As one of the few brown kids in school, and probably the most awkward and unattractive among them, I experienced an intense sort of alienation. I understood early in life the conditions of nor-mativity. It didn't take long to correspondingly understand the role of race, gender, class, sexuality, appearance, ethnicity, religion, and ideology in creating those conditions. I used to complain to Mom about xenophobia, though at the time I didn't know the word, only its meaning. She gave a response typical of overtaxed parents: others have it worse.

In this case, though, the response contained substance. Mom wasn't rebuffing my indignation, but imparting a crucial lesson about the hierarchies of American racism.

"Your father and I immigrated to this country, but we were able to live in a neighborhood that some people born here can't live in," she often explained. Bluefield's Black population wasn't huge, but it was significant. The town was almost fully segregated. The handful of immigrant families lived in white neighborhoods. All I could see from our vantage point was anti-Arab racism, but little of the rac-ist practices that allowed for our tenuous inclusion in the spaces of whiteness. I eventually realized Mom wasn't being melodramatic or recycling canards about the immigrant's extra burden, but attempt-ing to teach me about structural inequality. It is a lesson too little acknowledged in brown immigrant communities.

I wasn't oblivious to anti-Black racism; nobody in Bluefield could be. I just didn't understand my unwitting relationship with it or the ways it had benefitted my family (or at least exempted us from worse forms of marginalization). Anti-Black racism is deep-seated in Bluefield; not even strange newcomers with strange cus-toms and even stranger religions could unseat it. Since 9/11, folks around the country openly disparage Arabs and Muslims, but it's plain to see that much of the angst about Obama's secret ethnic or religious origin is unacknowledged anxiety about his Blackness.

I was twenty-three before I ever thought about North America as a colonized space. Sure, I had a vague sense that Bad Things

Happened® to Indians, but those histories were distant and abstract. Upon hearing that they weren't actually histories, but living realities, I finally comprehended why I so detested the commonplaces of schoolhouse bureaucracy: they developed from a colonial logic, with its attendant violence and inequality, of precisely the kind I could easily recognize in Palestine. Even Mom, the race-conscious guilt-tripper, had little sense of Indigenous sentience. And she's from Nicaragua, where Miskito, Rama, and Garifuna Indians were displaced by the same Sandinistas she reviled. Natives are the present absence of American identity.

My anti-authoritarianism merely needed a language. I feel lucky that I was able to find one, a process that will continue until I die. Part of our charge as educators is to encourage students to find the language that will help them translate instinct into concrete knowledge. It's the kind of preparation we all need to survive the capitalist marketplace. While anti-authoritarianism may start as an attitude, it has infinite capacity to develop into an ethic.

Distrusting the motivation of institutions and their managers often means demotion or recrimination, but if this sort of thing matters to you, it also means you'll never be wrong. There is reason to distrust authority on campus. Universities are lucrative spaces; nothing is lucrative without also being corrupt. As Thomas Frank puts it in his brilliant "Academy Fight Song":

> The coming of "academic capitalism" has been anticipated and praised for years; today it is here. Colleges and universities clamor greedily these days for pharmaceutical patents and ownership chunks of high-tech startups; they boast of being "entrepreneurial"; they have rationalized and outsourced countless aspects of their operations in the search for cash; they fight their workers nearly as ferociously as a nineteenth-century railroad baron; and the richest among them have turned their endowments into in-house hedge funds.

Frank later pinpoints the reason for campus authoritarianism:

> Above all, what the masters of academia spend the loot on is themselves. In saying this, I am not referring merely to the increasing number of university presidents who take home annual "compensation" north of a million dollars. That is a waste, of course, an outrageous bit of money-burning borrowed from Wall Street in an age when we ought to be doing the opposite of borrowing from Wall Street. But what has really fueled the student's ever-growing indebtedness, as anyone with a connection to academia can tell you, is the insane proliferation of university administrators.

The numbers validate Frank's observation. Benjamin Ginsberg points out that in the past thirty years, the administrator-to-student ratio has increased while the instructor-to-student ratio has stagnated. The rise of untenured, or non-tenure-track, faculty exacerbates the problem; a significant demographic in academe lacks job security or the working conditions that allow them to maximize their pedagogical talent. Over a recent ten-year period, spending on administration outpaced spending on instruction by 14 percent. At American universities, there are now more administrators and their staffers than full-time faculty.[44] In the past ten years, administrative salaries have steadily risen while custodians and groundskeepers suffer the inevitable budget cuts—as do the students whose tuition and fees supplement this largesse.

When so much money is at stake, those who raid the budget have a deep interest in maintaining the reputation of the institution. Their privilege and the condition of the brand are causally related. The brand thus predominates.

Its predominance often arrives at the expense of student well-being. The matter of sexual assault, for example, has lately emerged

---

44. Ginsberg presents these statistics in a *Washington Monthly* piece titled "Administrators Ate My Tuition."

(though the problem of sexual assault has been around for centuries). Studies suggest that more than three-quarters of victims know their attacker. Reporting rates have recently risen, but all versions of sexual assault remain woefully underreported.

There are numerous reasons why a victim chooses to keep silent. One reason is that she may expect a wholly inadequate, or even hostile, response from her own university. In 2014, Columbia University fielded twenty-eight federal complaints claiming the university had inadequately investigated reports of sexual assault. Florida State University, with the help of the Tallahassee Police Department, orchestrated a clumsy cover-up of a rape allegation to protect star quarterback Jameis Winston.[45] Speaking of sports, at the University of North Carolina–Chapel Hill, an administrator told rape survivor Annie Clark, "Rape is like football, and when you look back at the game, what would you have done differently in that situation."[46] Amherst College, which fancies itself above such lowbrow behavior as sports-related cover-ups, institutionalized a student who had spoken to counselors about her sexual assault. The student later withdrew from school.[47]

A different category of sexual assault infamously occurred at Pennsylvania State University, where the defensive coordinator of the football squad, Jerry Sandusky, was found to have molested vari-

45. Florida State also accepted money from the Koch brothers to hire a libertarian economist and appointed the former Republican speaker of the House, John Thrasher, as president. Thrasher is a creationist who has never worked in a university.
46. UNC is also dealing with a scandal in which athletes registered for hundreds of ghost courses.
47. Of her confinement the student says: "I felt like a prisoner, or, more accurately, like a harem girl. My jail was luxurious and open air, I was free to move about, the ruling power judged my worth on a weekly basis, and I was constantly reminded how lucky I was to be there." She also says, "Each time I met with my dean I felt more emotionally distraught than I had beforehand. Her comments reminded me that in the Administration's eyes I was the most base individual: a poor and parentless humanities major who was the school's token-Deep-Southerner. I was sullied, blameworthy, and possibly insane."

ous children, some of them on campus. We don't know the extent of the abuse because Sandusky ran a charity for at-risk youth, creating an elaborate pretext to maliciously exploit society's most vulnerable demographic. He thus rendered himself a community hero while pursuing his predations. Even after Sandusky had resigned from the football program, athletics administrators (and head coach Joe Paterno) provided him access to sporting facilities. Investigations suggest that even university president Graham Spanier was aware of Sandusky's behavior. The heavy hitters of the town and university, including Paterno and members of the board of Sandusky's charity, held common business investments.

For anybody who (rightly) views upper administrators as another class of capitalist management, Penn State's complicity in child molestation is but an extreme instance of a common phenomenon. Sandusky's terrible deeds surprised me, but not the overwhelming evidence that management, and Paterno himself, ignored Sandusky's depravity. Who gives a damn about destitute children systematically abused by a predator fully protected by the elite of his community when there are real estate deals to conduct and donations to deposit? These are the same folks who wax sanctimonious about the pure and principled endeavors of the universities they oversee.

If I might return to my "support the troops" imbroglio, I remember that as the controversy grew the Virginia Tech president's chief of staff, emulating her colleague Denis McDonough, undertook grand gestures of appeasement in responding to complaints. The loudest and most banal gesture, which made clear her affinities—along with, by extension, the president's—was but a simple line added to her bio, tucked among phone numbers and addresses: "Daughter of a World War II Veteran."

Apparently, the heroic trope of military service is inherited, but without taxation.

University spokesman Larry Hincker, second in command, was relentless, exalting Virginia Tech's unmatched military credentials, browbeating the community into one approved opinion, downgrading my academic rank, manipulating the word "murderer," extolling the university's integrity, tacitly apologizing for not being legally able to fire his errant ward.

His form letter to the disenchanted, spit-shining their jingoism, included a new honorific: "Vietnam era U.S. Navy veteran." The qualifier "era" implies that no service in Vietnam actually occurred, but either way it is a bio line with no reason for inclusion beyond the magic that mechanical support of the military can perform for those seeking patriotic credibility. (May his descendants proudly brandish the title.)

As the controversy raged, I met with Hincker, along with my department chair and dean. Hincker was in a helpful mood, assuring me that all would be well if I produced a statement clarifying my position. The chicanery of the request intimated a coalescence of corporation and university, with the state, as usual, obeying the corporations and embodying the universities. My department chair silently watched, later calling me repeatedly to confirm that I wouldn't in fact be releasing a clarification. In these moments, persistent obedience is a virtue.

To corporations, clarity is not a virtue. They thrive on the poetics of euphemism and treat truth as the verisimilitude of focus groups and consumer spending. Ambivalence and obeisance are their greatest assets. In this world of smirking plutocracy, clarifying a controversial statement means declaiming the substance of the controversy because clarification is supposed to comfort the powerful. Clarity in reaction to controversy is capitulation to the need of power to reassure itself of permanent reign.

I declined Hincker's offer and our stalemate resumed. He could understand, he assured me, my distorted idealism, my hyperbolic overreach. Why, he'd even been guilty of these things when he was young. When that didn't work, he spoke of soldiers as heroic innocents toting enlightenment to unloving places. It was all so silly I wondered if Hincker would tell me he was spat upon at an airport during the Vietnam War.

Of course he did.

In this era of neoliberal graft, universities barely pretend to care about the ideals upon which higher education was founded (though the ideas themselves are dubious and exclusionary). Sure, admins and PR wonks still prattle about dialogue and self-improvement and the life of the mind, but not even impressionable eighteen-year-olds believe the claptrap. They know just as well as their superiors that college is really about acquiring the mythical-but-measurable status conferred to them by a crisp sheet of cotton-bond paper.

Students, like all demographics, respond to discursive stimuli. As universities more and more resemble corporations in their governance, language, and outlook, students have become acutely brand conscious. Guardianship of the brand thus predominates and overwhelms the primacy of thought and analysis to which sites of education are nominally committed.

Students no longer enter into places of learning. They pay exorbitant prices to access the socioeconomic capital of affiliation with the most recognizable avatars, adorned magisterially with armor and pastoral creatures and Latin phrases.

Take that most sacred element of pedagogy, critical thinking. Many faculty, enamored as they are with the cartographies of their own gratification, don't know how to do it, never mind imparting instruction in the practice to those trying to learn it. (My conception of "critical thinking" includes acting in some way on the knowledge it produces, if only in the formulation of a dynamic ethical worldview.)

Critical thinking encompasses numerous definitions, but one of the greatest skills it provides is the ability to recognize bullshit.

In its better moments, it attempts to undermine whatever bullshit it recognizes. In short, if critical thinking is to be useful, it necessarily endows its practitioners with a reflexive desire to identify and understand the discourses, practices, beneficiaries, and disguises of power; in turn, it engenders a persistent focus on subversion.

This sort of focus is low on the list of what universities want from students, just as critical thinking is a terribly undesirable quality in the corporate world, much more damning than selfishness or sycophancy. Let us then be honest about critical thinking: on the tongues of cunning bureaucrats, it is little more than an additive to brand equity, the vainglorious pomp of smug, uptight automatons who like to use buzzwords in their PowerPoint presentations.

Critical thinking by faculty is even more undesirable. In research institutions, we are paid to generate prestige and to amass grant money; in teaching-centered colleges, we enjoy excess enrollments according to fine-tuned equations that maximize the student-teacher ratio. (In elite liberal arts colleges, we pamper the kids with simulations of parental affection.) Critical thinking is especially harmful to adjuncts, reliant as they are for income on the munificence of well-paid bosses who cultivate a distended assemblage of expendable employees.

Nowhere in our employment contracts does it say, "Challenge the unarticulated aspirations of the institution, especially when it acts as a conduit and expression of state violence; and please try your best to support justice for those on and off campus who are impoverished by neoliberalism." If we practice critical thinking, though, it is difficult to avoid these obligations.

Because of their high-minded rhetoric, it is tempting to believe that university managers care about ethics or maybe even about justice, but most managers care about neither. The exceptions, of course, deserve our praise—just don't poke around the highly ranked schools if you want to find them. The key to a successful managerial career isn't striving to be a good person, but developing enough instinct to cheat and charm in opportune moments.

Whatever independence can be acquired in academe requires a fundamental distrust of authority, be it abstract or explicit. The same is true of civic spaces in the United States. There were never pure epochs of uncorrupted democracy, but increasing corporate control disturbs greater sectors of American life, particularly on campus. The economies of injustice underline policymaking; those who make policy are therefore invested in the unjust.

There is no choice anymore but to distrust authority. Management can reward us if we behave, but those rewards lead to the disenfranchisement of other human beings. There are better ways to conduct the practices of education.

NINETEEN

Civilized Twitter

Andrew Jackson @CivilizeThe5: Indians have neither the intelligence, the industry, the moral habits, nor the desire of improvement . . . essential to any favorable change.

Menachem Begin @TheFirstTerrorist: The Palestinians are beasts walking on two legs.

Richard Nixon @TrickyDick: I won't mind one goddamn bit to have a little anti-Semitism if it's on that issue.

Theodore Roosevelt @TheBigStick: I don't go so far as to think that the only good Indians are dead Indians, but I believe nine out of ten are.

Golda Meir @MilwaukeeBornGM: There were no such thing as Palestinians . . . they didn't exist.

Winston Churchill @EmpireFalls: I do not admit, for instance, that a great wrong has been done to the Red Indians of America or the black people of Australia.

Thomas Jefferson @UVaPrez1: Free blacks are pests in society who are as incapable as children of taking care of themselves.

Yitzhak Rabin @ThePeacefulOne: We shall reduce the Arab population to a community of woodcutters and waiters.

Abraham Lincoln @TheAmericanMyth: I believe there is no right . . . of the free States to enter into the slave States, and interfere with the question of slavery at all.

Theodore Herzl @FoundingFather: Spirit the penniless population across the frontier by denying it employment.

Rafael Eitan @SabraShatila4ever: When we have settled the land, all the Arabs will be able to do about it will be to scurry around like drugged cockroaches in a bottle.

Woodrow Wilson @ThePhrasemaker: Any man who carries a hyphen about with him carries a dagger that he is ready to plunge into the vitals of this Republic.

Shimon Peres @TheGoodCop: We reject attempts to create a similarity between the Holocaust and the Armenian allegations. Nothing similar to the Holocaust occurred.

Ronald Reagan @TheGreatDissimulator: Republicans for fifty years have been telling voters the biggest threat in your life is minorities are going to hijack government.

@TrickyDick: Do you know maybe one black country that's well run?

@ThePeacefulOne: Break their bones.

@SabraShatila4ever: Force is all they do or ever will understand. We shall use the ultimate force until the Palestinians come crawling to us on all fours.

@TheBigStick: The most vicious cowboy has more moral principle than the average Indian.

@TheGreatDissimulator: If an individual wants to discriminate against Negroes or others in selling or renting his house, it is his right to do so.

@UVaPrez1: In imagination blacks are dull, tasteless, and anomalous.

@EmpireFalls: I am strongly in favour of using poisoned gas against uncivilised tribes.

TWENTY

The Darling That Can No Longer Be Defended

Israel's actions are more and more indefensible. Plenty of people defend the idea or the honor of Israel, but not the state's behavior. Copious historiography has put beyond doubt the horror of Israel's founding, at which point seven hundred thousand to eight hundred thousand Palestinians were displaced, an event more or less in line with the vision of Zionism's founders. Human rights organizations across the world have documented countless legal abuses and war crimes. Continued settlement of the West Bank renders proclamations about peace hollow and hypocritical. Open fascists grace the corridors of the Knesset. Leaders keep proposing or passing legislation that marginalizes non-Jews; more than fifty laws discriminate against Israel's Palestinian citizens. The peoples of the Third World, and increasing portions of the First World, view Israel as a symbol of colonial aggression.

The difficulty of defending Israel's actions partly accounts for the punitive measures its supporters inflict on the state's critics. Academic freedom cannot function when retribution fills the spaces of debate. There is plenty of room for moral and analytical disagreement around the Israel-Palestine conflict, but the facts of Israel's behavior are trenchant. Folks who recount those facts should never experience punishment or pressure. Those invested in racism or colonization have long defended their troublesome beliefs simply by refusing to question them—or allowing those beliefs to be questioned.

I'm fascinated by the discursive turns Israel's partisans have recently proffered. In disputes around the 2013 ASA boycott resolution, opponents barely defended Israeli policy. The same is true of 2014's Operation Protective Edge. This isn't to say they didn't argue heartily in Israel's defense; they simply didn't offer actual defenses of Israel's behavior. Instead, they put forward the principle that criticism of Israel is inherently unsavory. Or they merely blamed Israel's belligerence on the Palestinians.

Thus discussion of the ASA boycott was defined by matters of strategy and obligation. Is it appropriate to boycott any state's academic institutions? In particular, is it appropriate to boycott Israel's academic institutions? Is this sort of thing within the purview of a scholarly association? Why aren't we boycotting China or Iran? Rarely did boycott opponents claim that the conditions inspiring the resolution—the complicity of Israeli universities in widespread repression—were false or fantastical. They ignored Palestinian suffering and fretted about the potential impact on Israeli scholars, instead. They also contended that the resolution singled out Israel. Some argued that academic boycott, along with BDS more broadly, is but a stealthy way to destroy Israel.[48]

These remonstrations offered no real defense of Israel. Its us-

---

48. Norman Finkelstein proffered this argument in 2012, saying, "They don't want Israel. They think they're being very clever. They call it their three tiers. . . . We want the end of the occupation, we want the right of return, and we want equal rights for Arabs in Israel. And they think they are very clever, because they know the result of implementing all three is what? What's the result? You know and I know what's the result: there's no Israel."

ers positioned Israel as exceptional and then complained about the state being targeted for special criticism. (The first thing one learns about Palestine solidarity work is that it's always okay to single out Israel—if the point is to render the state beyond denunciation.) Neither did the anxieties about other bad countries constitute a defense of Israel. To the contrary, they signaled tacit acknowledgment of Israeli brutality. (Nobody cares more about the people of Tibet, Cuba, Iran, North Korea, and Syria than a Zionist responding to condemnation of Israel.) And fretting about the destruction of Israel is no defense, but a meager attempt to preserve an anachronistic idea. (This entire narrative is projection par excellence—Israel already destroyed Palestine, after all.)

The notion that so much death in Gaza is the responsibility of Palestinians is crude, and arguably racist, but interesting as a rhetorical technique. After an Israeli naval shell killed four Palestinian boys on a Gaza beach, Naftali Bennett exemplified the approach in this exchange with CNN's Wolf Blitzer:

BLITZER: As we speak, we're just getting these reports, awful reports, four Palestinian kids, playing on a beach, all of a sudden killed. An Israeli gun boat shell landed there. You've heard of these reports, right? Do you—do you—
BENNETT: I just heard about it this moment. I think it's terrible that Hamas is butchering its own children. I would never take my children and place them next to missile launchers. Here's what they're doing. Hamas is conducting massive self-genocide. They're taking women and children, placing them next to missile launchers, and shooting the missiles at Israel.
BLITZER: But these kids apparently were playing on a beach.
BENNETT: I'm telling you—I'll tell you where we find the missile launchers. We find them in hospitals, in schools, in homes. I myself am a former commando fighter. I saw it in Lebanon. You have a kitchen. You have a living room. And then you have the missile launcher room. What they're deliberately doing is seeking to kill as many Palestinians as possible in order to yell to the

world, help us. And this is cynical and cowardly. You know, if you want to conduct terror against Israelis, which is unacceptable, send fighters to do it. Don't send your women and children.
BLITZER: But they are not sending them. These are little children. They were just playing on the beach. And, clearly, you were—you were—the Israeli military was aiming for some sort of target that, in the process, there was what they used to call the Pentagon collateral damage. These are human beings, though.
BENNETT: Israel never targets civilians deliberately, period. What Israel does is defends itself. And when people shoot at us—just as you would do with your family. If someone's shooting at your family, you'll shoot back. If that coward is hiding behind his own children, they might get hit. This whole thing can go away in one moment. Hamas needs to do one thing, stop shooting.

Despite Bennett's argument being absurd past the point of grotesque, he gives us much to unpack, in no small part because less bellicose versions of this narrative dominated the rhetoric of Israel's supporters.

Let's start with his claim that "Israel never targets civilians deliberately, period." Bennett ignored Blitzer's question about the four boys on the beach for good reason, because the very subject of the interview belied Bennett's assertion, which is factually impossible. Beyond the four boys, we have mounds of evidence that Israel deliberately targets civilians. Fred Abrahams of Human Rights Watch noted that during Operation Protective Edge "the Israeli military carried out attacks on or near three well-marked schools where it knew hundreds of people were taking shelter, killing and wounding scores of civilians. Israel has offered no convincing explanation for these attacks on schools where people had gone for protection and the resulting carnage." B'Tselem, the Israeli Information Center for Human Rights in the Occupied Territories, reported that "during the fighting in Gaza, dozens of residences were bombed while residents were at home. [We have compiled lists of] members of families killed in their homes in 72 incidents of bombing or shelling. In these incidents, 547 people were killed, including 125 women under the age of 60, 250 minors, and 29 people over the age of 60." A report by the Palestinian Center for Human Rights in Gaza declared, "In the early morning of Tuesday, 08 July 2014, Israeli occupation forces escalated their military operations against the Gaza Strip. Israeli warplanes launched dozens of airstrikes targeting many civilian objects, including houses."

American military officials considered Israel's tactics to be indiscriminate, particularly in the Gaza City neighborhood of Shujaiya. Early in the operation, senior IDF officials ordered tank commanders "to open fire at anything that moves." A senior American officer suggested that "the only possible reason for doing that [deploying so much weaponry] is to kill a lot of people in as short a period of time as possible. It's not mowing the lawn. It's removing the topsoil."[49] Retired lieutenant general Robert Gard said, "Holy bejeezus. That rate of fire over that period of time is astonishing. If the figures are even half right, Israel's response was absolutely disproportionate."

The greatest counter to Bennett's audacious claim, however, is the fact that more than a thousand Palestinian civilians died during Protective Edge. I'm not a physicist, but it seems quite impossible that hundreds of civilians could perish if they weren't targeted by the war machinery of a state whose leaders deliberately ordered bombing runs. Presumably they didn't simply suffer simultaneous cardiac arrest. Say what you will about Protective Edge, but it's factually impossible to assert that Israel didn't target civilians; that assertion can be debated only if Israel never launched bombs into residential areas. Bennett justified those civilian deaths with a non-sequitur and all the moral awareness of a termite.

The illogic continued when Bennett proclaimed that "Hamas is butchering its own children." By "Hamas," Bennett actually meant

---

49. "Mowing the lawn" references a common phrase Israeli politicians and military brass use to describe bombing operations in Gaza. On July 18, 2014, an Israeli security minister upped the rhetoric by proclaiming, "We will do more than mow the lawn in Gaza. We will scorch it."

"Palestinians," a conflation common in Zionist discourse, intended to implicate an entire people in mindless aggression and thus create a rationale for their slaughter. His discourse illuminates the risible linguistic disjunctions that arise in justifications of warfare.

It's useful to explore Bennett's strange logic as an intellectual exercise, even if we can't take it seriously as an ethical proposition. Let's assume the clamoring about human shields and missile launcher rooms and toddlers dancing on boxes of munitions is true. (It would be an assumption without legitimate grounding.) Israeli leaders still choose to drop bombs on those children. They clearly deployed some sort of algorithm in which they decided the Palestinian child is worthy of death for the purpose of whatever political gain they may have derived from killing her. Blaming the Palestinian for putting the child in harm's way stops short of the moral reckoning necessary to account for the choice and its many consequences. A government doesn't get to kill children and then disavow itself of agency.

But for many Zionists, the Israeli government, no matter how powerful, appears to have no agency at all. It answers reluctantly to the terrible things the Palestinians force it to do. This inability to take responsibility for their own positions—or to even name those positions as tangible—illuminates the profound illogic Zionism requires of its acolytes.[50] Blaming Palestinians for Netanyahu's choices is yet another example of the inability to defend Israeli policies.

By the way, I have to give Bennett credit for his deep knowledge of the enemy. We don't like to admit it, but the missile launcher room is the lifeblood of every Arab household. My parents were a bit conservative, so our missile launcher room wasn't next to the nursery, but over by the master suite. Truth be told, it always made

---

50. Other disjunctions include the desire to call a state which grants rights based on biology a "democracy"; the notion that Israel is also the domain of those who have no desire to live there; and the rationalization of ethnic cleansing based on a genocide.

me feel a bit inauthentic, but I learned later in life that it's not a hard and fast cultural rule that the missile launcher room be located as close as possible to children. It made me feel much better about my identity. A few Arabs I know didn't even grow up with missile launcher rooms, but these tended to be the sellouts and assimilationists. In Gaza, where residential buildings are tall and close together, missile launcher rooms are extremely important, especially on the lower levels, because sometimes Palestinians just feel like firing rockets five feet across the alleyway into their neighbors' kitchen.

Did I mention that Naftali Bennett is Israel's minister of the economy?

Despite his bluster, Bennett didn't offer anything resembling an actual defense of Israel. He merely castigated the Palestinians. Not even Israel's most avid ideologues could defend the state as it murdered an average of ten children a day during Protective Edge.

These rhetorical conventions influence the volatility of Palestine in American academe. If the Palestinians must be blamed for all Israeli shortcomings, then humanization of Palestine necessarily evokes forms of self-reflection adverse to the reproduction of power. Civility is tenuous. It relies on the native's inability to make the colonizer any better.

TWENTY-ONE

Consumption

Every night for over a week, it was the same: We are on the second floor of the Tysons Corner Mall. It's typically busy, but foot traffic isn't overwhelming. Small groups of thirtysomethings and teenagers mill about with plastic bags and cups of Starbucks coffee. Their conversations generate a cavernous din in the uncushioned building.

Our son, as he always does in public, runs joyously toward all points of interest. Diana and I hold hands and watch. He catches sight of something downstairs and ambles to the rectangular opening.

I notice there's no railing. But he is already at the edge, peering over the unprotected aperture. I yell. Everybody looks at me with concern or annoyance. They don't see the child about to fall. I run. I am a madman. I stumble. I dive.

It is too late. He has tumbled. I watch him, in slow motion, fall to the tile floor below. I hear the thud. I scramble, screaming, frantic, but there is no stairwell or escalator. I'm trapped upstairs. Diana has disappeared. The mall patrons stare quizzically, some backing away a few steps.

I wake in the morning not having remembered but terribly disturbed, with a feeling of overwhelming affection for my son. After some coffee and conversation, I recall the event and recount it to Diana.

"You have to quit reading about Gaza," she finally tells me.

TWENTY-TWO

An Incivility Manifesto

1. We critically examine all definitional commonplaces.
2. We maintain an antagonistic relationship with administrators when they sell our institutions to outside donors and corporate interests.
3. We oppose the exploitation of contingent labor.
4. We challenge explicit or implicit racism, homophobia, sexism, transphobia, ableism, and classism wherever we encounter them.
5. We believe students are learners, not customers.
6. We maintain that education should supersede the profit motive.
7. We consider the free market a lazy rationale for bloated administrative salaries.
8. We decolonize rather than authenticate academic spaces.
9. We reject diversity and seek actual representation instead.
10. We demand justice for victims of sexual assault and the banishment of their perpetrators and administrative enablers.
11. We reaffirm the principles and practices of faculty governance.
12. We seek to extract our institutions from the subsidization of militarism and state repression.

13. We envision the public university as an accessible site of class mobility.

14. We recognize that "land grants" encroach on the historical territories of North America's Native nations.

15. We adhere to the boycott of Israeli academic institutions until they cease their direct and indirect contributions to weapons development and military occupation.

16. We deplore the dispossession of Indigenous peoples around the world, especially as it occurs with the imprimatur of academic objectivity.

17. We're not suckers, so please stop patronizing us with the genteel vocabularies of colonial racism. We've heard it before. As did our ancestors.

TWENTY-THREE

A Politics of the Child

I remember Lee Edelman's masterful *No Future: Queer Theory and the Death Drive* when reflecting on parenthood. Edelman argues that the constant glorification of the child, who occupies imagined categories, creates an inability to accommodate ways of being that do not conform to capitalist strictures. By investing the child with a finite reserve of innocence, we construct a future of procreative uplift, devoid of queer bodies and ideas.

Complementary to Edelman's argument is the notion of performing some sort of political function "for the children." We don't want them corrupted, exposed too early to the failures of humanity. In turn, we form policy around the mythological figure of the child. Or at least we justify policy around that figure.

It annoys me to no end. Nearly every time somebody puts forward an idea to restrict anything fun or dissentient, he does it for—who else?—the children. Nobody can cuss, fuck, drink, carouse, smoke, or get stoned. God forbid the children get wind of such things. And forget about rejecting authority or challenging our superiors. We wouldn't want to be a bad influence. You know, because the children.

The same thing happens when administrators fret about "students." These poor, precious creatures just can't handle horrible things like debate or analysis. They exist merely to be affirmed. Professors, then, mustn't fill their heads with ideas that undermine common wisdom, because that might make them uncomfortable—and everybody knows that unhappy consumers damage the brand.

Invoking "the children" (or "the students") is an acutely boring form of moralism, usually motivated either by cowardice or duplicity. It can be cowardly because "the children," who lack subjectivity in this schema, are made to assume responsibility for the adult's deficiencies. It can be duplicitous because it evokes an imaginary demographic to conceptualize the despotic as scrupulous. The children symbolize the moralist's own fears and desires. I can't take seriously a person who outsources responsibility for his aspirations to a powerless demographic.

Yet I find value in a politics of the child, especially when we approach children as deeply thoughtful beings with agency (and as long as we're decent enough not to exploit them). If we accept the proposition that children bear no responsibility for the ills of the world, then we implicitly assume the responsibility for human shortcomings. In turn, when we think of children, we needn't envision an abstract future because we already assess an intelligible (if vexing) present. The child may well be a creation of the adult imagination, but in creating the child an adult analyzes the conditions of the child's innocence, which often invert his or her own corruptions. On the day of my son's birth, when I vowed, "I will do well for this child," it was an aspiration toward a worldly ethics as much as it was a proclamation of fatherly responsibility.

I also find value in the analysis of parenthood as a physical reality. Humans are remarkably slow developers. From the moment of conception through the months of gestation and finally the stages of infancy, toddlerhood, preschool, and school age, it is many years before a human mammal becomes minimally competent at self-care. As such, parenting requires devotion. It is difficult for many parents to separate that devotion from their politics.

I cannot separate parenthood from politics. I think about Israeli parents who have lost children. I grieve for them. I empathize with them. It first seems like an instinctive act, a shared biological sensitivity, but it's also a political choice. It's possible to have feelings of affection for one's enemy while simultaneously recognizing the conditions that motivate territorial conflict. (I do not view the Israel-Palestine conflict as fundamentally ethnic or religious—colonization precedes ethnic or religious acrimony.) Anybody can be victim of those conditions, but those with less power are more likely to suffer violence. No colonial regime ever abjures violence, anyway.

The pain and fear Israelis profess is real to me. Even when I note that it comes at the expense of recognizing Palestinian humanity, as it often does, I understand that the feelings themselves exist and are legitimate by virtue of their very existence. Yet I see no happy future for Israelis and Palestinians unless the former acknowledge that their pain and fear aren't the pain and fear of the colonized. The colonizer's fear arises from the despair of the majoritarian. His pain derives from the regime's constant reliance on violence to shape national identity. I hear many Zionists worry not about the loss of life or livelihood, but about the deterioration of their institutional privilege.

Israelis who have lost loved ones grieve with deep emotion, as do Palestinians. This basic statement of mutual humanity should be the groundwork for creating a society in which both communities live in love and safety. Does it sound impossible? Of course it does. It probably is. But this is no reason to adopt a vision for the region in which one group (any group) remains permanently marginalized. Politically, socially, culturally, economically—we have to be more creative than the state, able to imagine ways of being that expand the limited options afforded us by neoliberalism.

The Nazi Holocaust is the great progenitor of Zionist pain and fear. I have no desire to degrade its importance to Israelis (and to Jews everywhere) or to critique how its victims and their descendants choose to heal. I can never fully understand what it means to be a part of this particular community, but I can work to appreciate its enormous shadow over modern Jewish peoplehood.

I do feel empowered to critique its political uses, though, because Israel's supporters frequently invoke it to justify Palestinian dispossession. In fact, Zionists don't always invoke the actual Holocaust, but an imagined second Holocaust at some undetermined date in the future to rationalize Israeli ethnocracy. The argument looks like this: "Jews need a safe place. If/when anti-Semitism rears its ugly head and Jews are endangered, we need a place to go, a place that is ours."

If I may speak directly to those who hold this belief:

I understand your anxiety. I really do. But do you realize how insensitive this argument sounds? Palestinians are supposed to languish in refugee camps and be deprived of civil and human rights so you can have a spare country just in case somebody like Hitler comes to power in the United States? (By the way, if this person ever comes to power he's most likely to emerge from the Christian Zionist community that mainstream Jewish leaders so eagerly court.) This anxiety about another Holocaust doesn't actually cohere to Israel's military occupation, which has nothing to do with keeping Jews safe and everything to do with grabbing land, money, and power. Please don't confuse a military economy with personal safety or cultural identity. Murdering hundreds of people in Gaza likewise has nothing to do with Jewish peoplehood. You've been tricked into thinking that your well-being is contingent on the misery of Palestinians.

I don't like ethnonationalism of any variety. I'm skeptical about the ability of the nation-state to act as a repository of justice. I oppose visions of Palestinian liberation that entail Jewish displacement. Oppression isn't something to be traded. A free Palestine means that all its citizens enjoy freedom. I don't make up this stuff; these ethics are hallmarks of Palestine's national liberation movement. They guide USACBI and the many activists who daily risk their lives inside and beyond Palestine.

A friend once defended me on Facebook to another person complaining about my "Israel bashing": "Salaita criticizes everything." It's true enough, when it comes to sites of authority, anyway. I've condemned the US government, Republicans, Democrats, Arab monarchies, Hamas, the Palestinian Authority, Bashar Assad, ISIS, John Kerry, the Catholic Church, the Muslim Brotherhood, David Cameron, CitiBank, the Free Syrian Army, Virginia Tech, Penn State, Barack Obama, the Red Cross, Hillary Clinton, the European Union, Goldman Sachs, Stephen Harper, the NYPD, Sisi, George W. Bush, JPMorgan Chase, the Tea Party, the Ivy League, and the Queen of England. At least I'm consistent. My detractors cite only tweets critical of Israel as inappropriate or uncivil.

Criticism of Israel has a unique ability to get one branded demonic or dangerous. There seems to be monstrous illogic in branding as bad those who deplore vicious state violence, but in the context of colonial discourse it's not illogical at all. Positioning oneself as steward of responsible critique by avoiding structures of injustice is paramount to the norms of respectability. Institutions and agents of the state constantly provide opportunities to affiliate with the respectable. They even allow us to pretend that the affiliation is voluntary. The makeup of nearly every high-paying gig in the country illustrates that supporting Israel isn't a career impediment in the United States.

It can be extraordinarily frustrating, yes. But the response is simple enough: we do not deplore Israel's deeds because we are bad people; we do so because we think deeply and often about what it means to be kind and empathetic.

There's one thing I remember most from the episodes of unmitigated Israeli brutality in Gaza: the ice cream freezers. Nothing affected me more. Few things better exemplify the gaiety and innocence of childhood than rummaging through boxes of frozen confections. During Israel's recent bombing campaign in Gaza, however, the ice cream freezers weren't stacked with popsicles and sorbet. Instead, they stored the bodies of dead children.

The symbolism is endless. Ice cream and children's bodies. They usually intermingle in messy harmony. This time, though, the bodies had replaced the treats. The children had nothing to imbibe. Their corpses were on display for a much different sort of rummaging.

They were in ice cream freezers because morgues had run out of space, a problem not only of warfare but of overcrowded neighborhoods and geographical entrapment. Gaza's lack of electricity threatened rapid decomposition. The children rested atop one another in containers that likely provided some of their happiest moments when they were alive.

There is nothing poetic about this juxtaposition. It is a terrible algorithm of combustion and confinement.

Thus I tweeted.

The evidence in my case is clear: I am no anti-Semite. I am no terrorist. I am no bully. I am no savage. I am a man who was fired because I condemned Israeli policy in language appropriate to a horrible occasion rather than in the meek platitudes of civility. I prefer moral clarity. After all, there is nothing civil about dead children in an ice cream freezer.

Speaking in Times of Repression

What to do about injustice? How to counter it while attempting to put food in our bodies? These are questions for which I have no solid answers.

I hear these inquiries a lot lately. I do not resent them. I admire the minds from which they emerge. All humans are well served considering such questions. I'm simply not very good at answering them.

The first thing to recognize is that it has always been a time of repression. Find who profits from the existence of injustice. When you do, you'll have simultaneously discovered its cause and solution.

This observation tells us nothing of process. We have answers to every social ill. We don't own the means to implement those answers.

I embody a contradiction between personal and political belief. My instinct, which I fully understand isn't actually instinctive, is simply to tell people to do what they feel comfortable doing. I'm not big on demands or injunctions. It's anathema to my lifelong desire to be left alone. Yet I recognize that as somebody who now exists in a public position I will be summoned to analyze a set of dynamics in which I and UIUC are embroiled. These dynamics are especially important to folks in academe who wish to pursue material commitments alongside theoretical and philosophical questions.

Graduate students and prospective graduate students are especially anxious these days. They are right to be. Because of corporatized campuses and the attendant de-emphasis of non-revenue-producing fields, decent humanities jobs are in decline.[51] Grad school slots have become more competitive. Any advantage is a great asset. Being deemed a troublemaker or a radical is no advantage.

Making trouble is precisely the function of the intellectual, though. And being radical is a solid antidote to boring work.

There's always been repression and recrimination in academe. Anybody with an eye toward a career as a scholar has to internalize this reality in his or her decision-making process. Aspiring and established scholars should not abdicate intellectual commitments in order to please those comfortable only with orthodoxy. This would be careerism, not inquiry.

And that's the point. If we don't examine relationships of power and highlight the disjunctions of inequality, then we're not doing our jobs. (We will be according to the preferences of the managerial class, but pleasing its functionaries isn't generally the mark of an interesting thinker.) Reading the world in ways that contravene the propriety of the civil isn't extraneous to our labor, but the primary impetus for it. I would advise anybody considering taking up the life of an intellectual that upsetting arbiters of common sense is an immanent feature of useful scholarship.

I therefore distinguish between producing solid scholarship and vocally assuming an activist position (by, say, organizing panels, working with a union, spouting off on social media, publishing in opinion journals, joining demonstrations, and so forth). Silence, remember, is a form of communication, sometimes with damning outcomes. There are countless ways to pursue justice on campus.

---

51. There is some evidence that the profitability of the STEM fields is a myth.

Some are no more complex than being a good teacher and an honest mentor. Others require only that we act in community rather than adhering to the individualistic cultures of capitalism and colonization. If assuming a public posture is something you want to do, though, then fear shouldn't be a hindrance.

I suppose I'm trying to say: if you feel called to speak, it is okay to be scared; but don't be silent.

Ultimately, speaking publicly in support of the wretched is a deeply personal choice. Individual situations differ. One person may be in a better position to handle recrimination than another. Those with family money or powerful connections have the luxury to rabble-rouse that doesn't exist for the single mother or the immigrant who sends her paycheck back home. People of color are more likely to be criminalized for dissent than their white counterparts. "What can/should we do?" is not a universal question.

Consider also that the labor of minority scholars is already politicized. We have to publish more. It's risky to be introverted because so many white colleagues cannot tolerate a minority who doesn't pretend to like them. We have to act as diversity representative on all sorts of committees. We cannot be mediocre because our tenure and upward mobility rely on senior colleagues who reward only their own mediocrity. It's hazardous for us to show emotion because we're aware of the possibility of confirming to others our innate unreason. Adding "activist leader" to this list of tasks is a heavy undertaking. In many ways, simply deciding not to appease power is an active form of advocacy. It is the activism of survival.

I know that many students and scholars of Palestinian origin feel compelled to act. To them I say:

Do not fear the pro-Israel activist industry. Yes, they have inordinate resources and influence. And, yes, their actions can be vicious. But suppression is not a long-term strategy. It's the tactic of one whose ideology has no merit beyond the force he can summon to impose it on those with less power.

Please do not misread me: Israel's supporters, as they have illustrated for many decades, are content to rely on suppression as long as it can effectively preserve their colonial fetish, no matter how many constitutional rights they destroy.

Suppression relies on the anxiety of its targets. It is sustainable, then, only in relation to our quiescence.

Nobody should stop you from articulating a principled critique of unjust power. When that unjust power is Zionism, the impetus to act is even greater, for in so doing we also respond to American colonization, restricted speech, racism, neoliberalism, militarization, ethnocracy, and a host of related issues about which those in our profession should be concerned.

Pro-Israel operatives rely on our fear to embolden their tactics of intimidation. It is no small comfort that they fear our mere existence much more, however.

It's really a matter of where we choose to locate our commitments. When it comes to systematic critique of Israel, somebody is going to be punished. If you are unwilling to be that person, then keep a lower profile until such time as you may be ready. In the meantime, there is still plenty to do. For faculty:

- Attend relevant events on campus. A large audience provides a great visual and even greater opportunities for productive interchange.
- Support student activists. They assume tremendous risk, including expulsion and police violence. Advise them. Don't allow them to take all the heat.
- Organize. Every time somebody stands in front of a microphone, it requires considerable organization. If you don't want to be the one in front of that microphone, then consider being one of the organizers.
- Vote in the elections of scholarly associations. Various ref-

erenda about Palestine have been presented across numerous disciplines for member approval in the past ten years, with many more to come. A low percentage of membership traditionally participates in these elections. Voting is a virtually risk-free way to provide an impact.

- Investigate your school's study abroad program. If there is an arrangement with an Israeli university, it may contravene the school's policies of inclusion because Arab or Muslim students could be denied the opportunity to participate due to Israel's discrimination at the borders it controls.

- Hold your university accountable to its inclusionary rhetoric as it pertains to the suppression of Palestinian voices. Write or visit relevant parties about the racism implicit to concerns about Arab or Muslim civility.

- Keep in mind: a mealy mouth isn't the same thing as diplomacy.

For contingent/untenured faculty:

- See the list above and select according to your circumstances. Above all, demand that those who have the protections of tenure make use of them rather than chasing shitty merit raises or zealously proving their civility.

For students:

- Hold your superiors to account for their high-minded rhetoric.

- Never trust a grinning administrator who tells you he has your best interest in mind.

- When you get called into a meeting with the dean, lawyer up.

- It's your campus, too. Cede it to nobody.

- Seek out sympathetic faculty. Let them know what you're doing. Invite them to your events. Many have no idea what's happening on campus.

- Document everything.

- Whenever a pro-Israel group approaches you to "dialogue," consider it a surefire indication that you're winning. Ignore the request. In this instance, "dialogue" means appropriation.
- Develop relationships with local business owners who are sympathetic. You can help bring them customers; they can help provide you food or materials.
- Keep being brilliant. You're exactly the type of student every decent professor dreams of teaching—the type, that is, from whom we constantly learn.

There's so much more. Creative organizing is infinite. I feel silly making lists, to be honest. Getting fired doesn't make me an expert on anything. I'm doing my best to make sure something productive comes of it, though. To be less oblique: I hope my firing manages in some way to advance the cause of Palestine on or off campus. By extension, I hope engagement with Palestine manages to advance the cause of North American decolonization.

If you want to support me, support the people of Palestine; support Natives still dispossessed of land and resources; support African Americans brutalized by the police; support anybody subject to systematic state violence. My having a job changes nothing if the system that orchestrated my ouster remains intact. I am merely a symbol of the stark imperatives of the wealthy and well connected. We all are, really. Unless the system changes at a basic level, everybody is merely buying shares in a neoliberal corporation with the power to dissolve our interests the moment we become an inconvenience.

Arabs and Jews sometimes talk of our commonalities. Even in moments of hostility, we can acknowledge, if only grudgingly, a set of cultural or historical affinities. That's how I know the remonstration around process in my termination is disingenuous. Zionists and anti-Zionists understand full well why I was fired: because I criticized Israel too loudly. Everything else is secondary.

Here's the most important commonality, though, one we rarely discuss: in the United States and Canada (and Latin America), Arabs and Jews are both settlers. An issue that inspires such heated debate in the Holy Land hasn't even a whimper of controversy in North America. Arab and Jewish Americans simultaneously occupy Native lands. And the majority of us have benefitted from an elusion of Blackness. Our trajectories in the United States have been pretty different. Now, Arabs are firmly ensconced as people of color while most Jews have achieved the status of white. The consequences of this difference are enormous. Yet the fundamental commonality remains.

That commonality provides an impetus for us to work in community to dismantle the ongoing systems of colonization in North America (and the Pacific and the Caribbean). Those systems entail a longstanding racism of which we have been both victim and beneficiary. We shouldn't push for solidarity solely in relation to Palestine, but also in conversation with the first casualties of American empire. These relationships must presuppose a commitment to justice in the Holy Land.

There is much, then, to keep us busy. I have no desire to judge another person's form or level of commitment. Do as you wish and as your resources allow. I repeat, though, that there is nothing to fear but the oppressor's power only as we have internalized it by being educated in his self-image.

In short:

As long as African Americans continue to endure, despite police violence and gerrymandering and voter disenfranchisement and redlining and disproportionate incarceration and housing discrimination and underfunded schools and majoritarian microaggression and a racist legal system; as long as Indigenous peoples continue to endure, despite land expropriation and intellectual theft and exile and mass murder and treaty violations and environmental destruction and mascotry and programs of assimilation and being written out of history; as long as the poor of the world continue to endure, despite non-potable water and inadequate housing and First World do-gooderism and sexual violence and wage slavery (and physical slavery) and scarcity and shanties and slumlords and starvation; as long as Palestinians continue to endure, despite military occupation and demonization and checkpoints and land theft and foreign settlement and Israeli bombs and geographical entrapment and refugee camps and third-class citizenship and carceral brutality; as long as all people who suffer continue to endure, despite the dangers of endurance,

So, too, must we.

EPILOGUE

Just as this manuscript was going to press, my conflict with UIUC took some dramatic turns. On August 6, 2015, federal judge Harry D. Leinenweber of the Seventh Circuit (Northern Illinois) ruled on the university's motion to dismiss my lawsuit. While he rejected my claims of tortious interference (which implicated anonymous donors) and spoliation (which implicated Phyllis Wise for destroying evidence), he emphatically endorsed the argument that I had a valid employment contract and that UIUC violated my speech rights.

The same afternoon, in a move that shocked many observers, Wise resigned as chancellor of UIUC, strongly alluding to the controversy around my firing without directly referencing it. Wise's $400,000 severance package came under intense criticism, though also noteworthy was her move into a faculty position worth approximately $300,000. Her first year on faculty will be spent on paid sabbatical.

The following day, the university released the first batch of email correspondence queued up from several FOIA requests. The correspondence validated even the most cynical suspicions of the university's detractors. I hesitate to offer any sort of analysis that reads as conclusive because it's clear this story is only beginning. Here are some of the things we learned from the first batch of messages:

- University officials offered numerous public statements that contravened what was actually happening behind the scenes.

- Wise and her cronies worked hard to exclude relevant faculty bodies and ignore university statutes.
- The desire for a new medical school in Urbana, opposed by power brokers in Chicago and some local residents who would be affected, inspired much of the action.
- Wise often lobbied leaders of the local business community.
- Participants articulated disdain for the American Indian Studies Program, and for the humanities more broadly.
- Participants sometimes debated academic freedom, but mainly to find a post hoc rationale for their violations of the practice.
- Provost Ilesanmi Adesida played a much larger role than observers were led to believe.
- Wise insinuated that she was ordered to act from above and was subsequently made to "carry the water."
- The interactions between Wise and the board of trustees sometimes appeared to be tense.
- Nick Burbules and Joyce Tolliver instigated or endorsed many of Wise's stupidest decisions. Wise apparently vetted the *News-Gazette* op-ed coauthored by Burbules and Tolliver in which they called for "honest debate."
- Wise wanted the search to replace Robert Easter as system president to fail, perhaps because of her own covetousness.
- Numerous parties in the exchanges conspired to avoid FOIA revelations.
- Wise tells the truth at least once: "This place is so messed up."

Just as UIUC's violations of law and abrogation of academic freedom required the assistance of a cross-range of participants, the fight to restore justice in the face of spectacular malfeasance has been a collaborative effort involving adjuncts, students, activists, tenured faculty, civil libertarians, attorneys, and journalists. Upper administrators across the country remain silent.

I had long suspected that ugly behavior would be exposed if I could endure the abuse and acrimony that always accompany challenges to institutional power. Here the reliance on collaboration is crucial. It takes people in community to expose corruption. I am profoundly grateful to the many people across the world who refused to leave me dispossessed. By availing myself of their support I've been able to withstand the persistent nastiness of Israel's and UIUC's apologists.

A final thought, if the reader is kind enough to entertain a bit of whimsy. Pushing back against the elite is risky: one can be criminalized, humiliated, insulted, and abandoned, as can one's family. Agents of power, usually pretending they're restoring order in the world, will do anything to discredit an agitator. Yet it's often worthwhile to push back. When we gamble on the cluelessness, hubris, and avarice of the powerful, then it doesn't take long to identify the eminently collapsible structures they inhabit. Be steadfast and persistent. Behave ethically. Invoke the dignity of children and ancestors. Accept the love and support of friends. Then wait for the elite to do the only thing at which they truly excel: undertake any action necessary to preserve their self-interest, including the cannibalization of supposed friends and allies and the destruction of the same institutions from which they generated their power and wealth.

Don't let anybody convince you the unjust exercise of power is complicated. Get beyond the tawdriness of the expensive clothes, mahogany tables, imperious titles, well-appointed offices, and shiny baubles we're continually socialized to deify, and you're left with something amusingly simple: sub-mediocre sycophants and inheritors of privilege who display all the psychological complexity of a mosquito buzzing around your ankles.

AAUP Statements

1940 Statement
of Principles
on Academic Freedom and Tenure

WITH 1970 INTERPRETIVE COMMENTS

In 1940, following a series of joint conferences begun in 1934, represen-
tatives of the American Association of University Professors and of the
Association of American Colleges (now the Association of American Col-
leges and Universities) agreed upon a restatement of principles set forth
in the 1925 Conference Statement on Academic Freedom and Tenure.
This restatement is known to the profession as the 1940 Statement of
Principles on Academic Freedom and Tenure.

The 1940 Statement is printed below, followed by Interpretive
Comments as developed by representatives of the American Association of
University Professors and the Association of American Colleges in 1969.
The governing bodies of the two associations, meeting respectively in No-
vember 1989 and January 1990, adopted several changes in language in
order to remove gender-specific references from the original text.

The purpose of this statement is to promote public understanding and support of academic freedom and tenure and agreement upon procedures to ensure them in colleges and universities. Institutions of higher education are conducted for the common good and not to further the interest of either the individual teacher or the institution as a whole.[1] The common good depends upon the free search for truth and its free exposition.

Academic freedom is essential to these purposes and applies to both teaching and research. Freedom in research is fundamental to the advancement of truth. Academic freedom in its teaching aspect is fundamental for the protection of the rights of the teacher in teaching and of the student to freedom in learning. It carries with it duties correlative with rights.[1][2]

Tenure is a means to certain ends; specifically: (1) freedom of teaching and research and of extramural activities, and (2) a sufficient degree of economic security to make the profession attractive to men and women of ability. Freedom and economic security, hence, tenure, are indispensable to the success of an institution in fulfilling its obligations to its students and to society.

ACADEMIC FREEDOM

1. Teachers are entitled to full freedom in research and in the publication of the results, subject to the adequate performance of their other academic duties; but research for pecuniary return should be based upon an understanding with the authorities of the institution.

2. Teachers are entitled to freedom in the classroom in discussing their subject, but they should be careful not to introduce into their teaching controversial matter which has

---

1. The word "teacher" as used in this document is understood to include the investigator who is attached to an academic institution without teaching duties.
2. Boldface numbers in brackets refer to Interpretive Comments that follow.

no relation to their subject.[2] Limitations of academic freedom because of religious or other aims of the institution should be clearly stated in writing at the time of the appointment.[3]

3. College and university teachers are citizens, members of a learned profession, and officers of an educational institution. When they speak or write as citizens, they should be free from institutional censorship or discipline, but their special position in the community imposes special obligations. As scholars and educational officers, they should remember that the public may judge their profession and their institution by their utterances. Hence they should at all times be accurate, should exercise appropriate restraint, should show respect for the opinions of others, and should make every effort to indicate that they are not speaking for the institution.[4]

ACADEMIC TENURE

After the expiration of a probationary period, teachers or investigators should have permanent or continuous tenure, and their service should be terminated only for adequate cause, except in the case of retirement for age, or under extraordinary circumstances because of financial exigencies.

In the interpretation of this principle it is understood that the following represents acceptable academic practice:

1. The precise terms and conditions of every appointment should be stated in writing and be in the possession of both institution and teacher before the appointment is consummated.

2. Beginning with appointment to the rank of full-time instructor or a higher rank,[5] the probationary period should not exceed seven years, including within this period full-time service in all institutions of higher education; but subject to

the proviso that when, after a term of probationary service of more than three years in one or more institutions, a teacher is called to another institution, it may be agreed in writing that the new appointment is for a probationary period of not more than four years, even though thereby the person's total probationary period in the academic profession is extended beyond the normal maximum of seven years.[6] Notice should be given at least one year prior to the expiration of the probationary period if the teacher is not to be continued in service after the expiration of that period.[7]

3. During the probationary period a teacher should have the academic freedom that all other members of the faculty have.[8]

4. Termination for cause of a continuous appointment, or the dismissal for cause of a teacher previous to the expiration of a term appointment, should, if possible, be considered by both a faculty committee and the governing board of the institution. In all cases where the facts are in dispute, the accused teacher should be informed before the hearing in writing of the charges and should have the opportunity to be heard in his or her own defense by all bodies that pass judgment upon the case. The teacher should be permitted to be accompanied by an advisor of his or her own choosing who may act as counsel. There should be a full stenographic record of the hearing available to the parties concerned. In the hearing of charges of incompetence the testimony should include that of teachers and other scholars, either from the teacher's own or from other institutions. Teachers on continuous appointment who are dismissed for reasons not involving moral turpitude should receive their salaries for at least a year from the date of notification of dismissal whether or not they are continued in their duties at the institution.[9]

5. Termination of a continuous appointment because of financial exigency should be demonstrably bona fide.

1940 INTERPRETATIONS

At the conference of representatives of the American Association of University Professors and of the Association of American Colleges on November 7–8, 1940, the following interpretations of the 1940 Statement of Principles on Academic Freedom and Tenure were agreed upon:

1. That its operation should not be retroactive.
2. That all tenure claims of teachers appointed prior to the endorsement should be determined in accordance with the principles set forth in the 1925 Conference Statement on Academic Freedom and Tenure.
3. If the administration of a college or university feels that a teacher has not observed the admonitions of paragraph 3 of the section on Academic Freedom and believes that the extramural utterances of the teacher have been such as to raise grave doubts concerning the teacher's fitness for his or her position, it may proceed to file charges under paragraph 4 of the section on Academic Tenure. In pressing such charges, the administration should remember that teachers are citizens and should be accorded the freedom of citizens. In such cases the administration must assume full responsibility, and the American Association of University Professors and the Association of American Colleges are free to make an investigation.

1970 INTERPRETIVE COMMENTS

Following extensive discussions on the 1940 Statement of Principles on Academic Freedom and Tenure with leading educational associations and with individual faculty members and administrators, a joint committee of the AAUP and the Association of American Colleges met during 1969 to reevaluate this key policy statement. On the basis of the comments received, and the discussions that ensued, the joint committee felt the preferable approach was to formulate interpretations of the Statement in terms of the experience gained in implementing and applying the Statement for over thirty years and of adapting it to current needs.

The committee submitted to the two associations for their consideration the following "Interpretive Comments." These interpretations were adopted by the Council of the American Association of University Professors in April 1970 and endorsed by the Fifty-sixth Annual Meeting as Association policy.

In the thirty years since their promulgation, the principles of the 1940 Statement of Principles on Academic Freedom and Tenure have undergone a substantial amount of refinement. This has evolved through a variety of processes, including customary acceptance, understandings mutually arrived at between institutions and professors or their representatives, investigations and reports by the American Association of University Professors, and formulations of statements by that association either alone or in conjunction with the Association of American Colleges. These comments represent the attempt of the two associations, as the original sponsors of the 1940 Statement, to formulate the most important of these refinements. Their incorporation here as Interpretive Comments is based upon the premise that the 1940 Statement is not a static code but a fundamental document designed to set a framework of norms to guide adaptations to changing times and circumstances.

Also, there have been relevant developments in the law itself reflecting a growing insistence by the courts on due process within the academic community which parallels the essential concepts of the 1940 Statement; particularly relevant is the identification by the Supreme Court of academic freedom as a right protected by the First Amendment. As the Supreme Court said in *Keyishian v. Board of Regents*, 385 U.S. 589 (1967), "Our Nation is deeply committed to safeguarding academic freedom, which is of transcendent value to all of us and not merely to the teachers concerned. That freedom is therefore a special concern of the First Amendment, which does not tolerate laws that cast a pall of orthodoxy over the classroom."

The numbers refer to the designated portion of the 1940 Statement on which interpretive comment is made.

1. The Association of American Colleges and the American Association of University Professors have long recognized that membership in the academic profession carries with it special responsibilities. Both associations either separately or jointly have consistently affirmed these responsibilities in major policy statements, providing guidance to professors in their utterances as citizens, in the exercise of their responsibilities to the institution and to students, and in their conduct when resigning from their institution or when undertaking government-sponsored research. Of particular relevance is the Statement on Professional Ethics, adopted in 1966 as Association policy. (A revision, adopted in 1987, may be found in AAUP, *Policy Documents and Reports*, 10th ed. [Washington, D.C., 2006], 171–72.)

2. The intent of this statement is not to discourage what is "controversial." Controversy is at the heart of the free academic inquiry which the entire statement is designed to foster. The passage serves to underscore the need for teachers to avoid persistently intruding material which has no relation to their subject.

3. Most church-related institutions no longer need or desire the departure from the principle of academic freedom

implied in the 1940 Statement, and we do not now endorse such a departure.

4. This paragraph is the subject of an interpretation adopted by the sponsors of the 1940 Statement immediately following its endorsement which reads as follows:

> If the administration of a college or university feels that a teacher has not observed the admonitions of paragraph 3 of the section on Academic Freedom and believes that the extramural utterances of the teacher have been such as to raise grave doubts concerning the teacher's fitness for his or her position, it may proceed to file charges under paragraph 4 of the section on Academic Tenure. In pressing such charges, the administration should remember that teachers are citizens and should be accorded the freedom of citizens. In such cases the administration must assume full responsibility, and the American Association of University Professors and the Association of American Colleges are free to make an investigation.

Paragraph 3 of the section on Academic Freedom in the 1940 Statement should also be interpreted in keeping with the 1964 *Committee A Statement on Extramural Utterances*, which states inter alia: "The controlling principle is that a faculty member's expression of opinion as a citizen cannot constitute grounds for dismissal unless it clearly demonstrates the faculty member's unfitness for his or her position. Extramural utterances rarely bear upon the faculty member's fitness for the position. Moreover, a final decision should take into account the faculty member's entire record as a teacher and scholar."

Paragraph 5 of the Statement on Professional Ethics also deals with the nature of the "special obligations" of the teacher. The paragraph reads as follows:

As members of their community, professors have the rights and obligations of other citizens. Professors measure the urgency of these obligations in the light of their responsibilities to their subject, to their students, to their profession, and to their institution. When they speak or act as private persons, they avoid creating the impression of speaking or acting for their college or university. As citizens engaged in a profession that depends upon freedom for its health and integrity, professors have a particular obligation to promote conditions of free inquiry and to further public understanding of academic freedom.

Both the protection of academic freedom and the requirements of academic responsibility apply not only to the full-time probationary and the tenured teacher, but also to all others, such as part-time faculty and teaching assistants, who exercise teaching responsibilities.

5. The concept of "rank of full-time instructor or a higher rank" is intended to include any person who teaches a full-time load regardless of the teacher's specific title.[3]

6. In calling for an agreement "in writing" on the amount of credit given for a faculty member's prior service at other institutions, the Statement furthers the general policy of full understanding by the professor of the terms and conditions of the appointment. It does not necessarily follow that a professor's tenure rights have been violated because of the absence of a written agreement on this matter. Nonetheless, especially because of the variation in permissible institutional practices, a written understanding concerning these matters at the time of appointment is particularly

---

3. For a discussion of this question, see the "Report of the Special Committee on Academic Personnel Ineligible for Tenure," *Policy Documents and Reports*, 9th ed. (Washington, DC, 2001), 88–91.

appropriate and advantageous to both the individual and the institution.[4]

7. The effect of this subparagraph is that a decision on tenure, favorable or unfavorable, must be made at least twelve months prior to the completion of the probationary period. If the decision is negative, the appointment for the following year becomes a terminal one. If the decision is affirmative, the provisions in the 1940 Statement with respect to the termination of service of teachers or investigators after the expiration of a probationary period should apply from the date when the favorable decision is made.

The general principle of notice contained in this paragraph is developed with greater specificity in the "Standards for Notice of Nonreappointment," endorsed by the Fiftieth Annual Meeting of the American Association of University Professors (1964). These standards are:

Notice of nonreappointment, or of intention not to recommend reappointment to the governing board, should be given in writing in accordance with the following standards:

1. *Not later than March 1 of the first academic year of service,* if the appointment expires at the end of that year; or, if a one-year appointment terminates during an academic year, at least three months in advance of its termination.

2. *Not later than December 15 of the second academic year of service,* if the appointment expires at the end of that year; or, if an initial two-year appointment terminates during an academic year, at least six months in advance of its termination.

---

4. For a more detailed statement on this question, see "On Crediting Prior Service Elsewhere as Part of the Probationary Period," *Policy Documents and Reports,* 10th ed. (Washington, DC, 2006), 55–56.

3. At least twelve months before the expiration of an appointment after two or more years in the institution.

Other obligations, both of institutions and of individuals, are described in the *Statement on Recruitment and Resignation of Faculty Members*, as endorsed by the Association of American Colleges and the American Association of University Professors in 1961.

8. The freedom of probationary teachers is enhanced by the establishment of a regular procedure for the periodic evaluation and assessment of the teacher's academic performance during probationary status. Provision should be made for regularized procedures for the consideration of complaints by probationary teachers that their academic freedom has been violated. One suggested procedure to serve these purposes is contained in the *Recommended Institutional Regulations on Academic Freedom and Tenure*, prepared by the American Association of University Professors.

9. A further specification of the academic due process to which the teacher is entitled under this paragraph is contained in the "Statement on Procedural Standards in Faculty Dismissal Proceedings," jointly approved by the American Association of University Professors and the Association of American Colleges in 1958. This interpretive document deals with the issue of suspension, about which the 1940 Statement is silent.

The 1958 Statement provides: "Suspension of the faculty member during the proceedings is justified only if immediate harm to the faculty member or others is threatened by the faculty member's continuance. Unless legal considerations forbid, any such suspension should be with pay." A suspension which is not followed by either reinstatement or the opportunity for a hearing is in effect a summary dismissal in violation of academic due process.

The concept of "moral turpitude" identifies the exceptional case in which the professor may be denied a year's teaching or pay in whole or in part. The statement applies to that kind of behavior which goes beyond simply warranting discharge and is so utterly blameworthy as to make it inappropriate to require the offering of a year's teaching or pay. The standard is not that the moral sensibilities of persons in the particular community have been affronted. The standard is behavior that would evoke condemnation by the academic community generally.

Statement on Professional Ethics

The statement that follows, a revision of a statement originally adopted in 1966, was approved by the Association's Committee on Professional Ethics, adopted by the Association's Council in June 1987, and endorsed by the Seventy-third Annual Meeting.

INTRODUCTION

From its inception, the American Association of University Professors has recognized that membership in the academic profession carries with it special responsibilities. The Association has consistently affirmed these responsibilities in major policy statements, providing guidance to professors in such matters as their utterances as citizens, the exercise of their responsibilities to students and colleagues, and their conduct when resigning from an institution or when undertaking sponsored research. The Statement on Professional Ethics that follows sets forth those general standards that serve as a reminder of the variety of responsibilities assumed by all members of the profession.

In the enforcement of ethical standards, the academic profession differs from those of law and medicine, whose associations act to ensure the integrity of members engaged in private practice. In the academic profession the individual institution of higher learning provides this assurance and so should normally handle questions concerning propriety of conduct within its own framework by reference to a faculty group. The Association supports such local action and stands ready, through the general secretary and the Committee on Professional Ethics, to counsel with members of the academic community concerning questions of professional ethics and to inquire into complaints when local consideration is impossible or inappropriate. If the alleged offense is deemed sufficiently serious to raise the possibility of adverse action, the procedures should be in accordance with the 1940 Statement of Principles on Academic Freedom and Tenure, the 1958 Statement on Procedural Standards in Faculty Dismissal Proceedings, or the applicable provisions of the Association's Recommended Institutional Regulations on Academic Freedom and Tenure.

THE STATEMENT

1. Professors, guided by a deep conviction of the worth and dignity of the advancement of knowledge, recognize the special responsibilities placed upon them. Their primary responsibility to their subject is to seek and to state the truth as they see it. To this end professors devote their energies to developing and improving their scholarly competence. They accept the obligation to exercise critical self-discipline and judgment in using, extending, and transmitting knowledge. They practice

intellectual honesty. Although professors may follow subsidiary interests, these interests must never seriously hamper or compromise their freedom of inquiry.

2. As teachers, professors encourage the free pursuit of learning in their students. They hold before them the best scholarly and ethical standards of their discipline. Professors demonstrate respect for students as individuals and adhere to their proper roles as intellectual guides and counselors. Professors make every reasonable effort to foster honest academic conduct and to ensure that their evaluations of students reflect each student's true merit. They respect the confidential nature of the relationship between professor and student. They avoid any exploitation, harassment, or discriminatory treatment of students. They acknowledge significant academic or scholarly assistance from them. They protect their academic freedom.

3. As colleagues, professors have obligations that derive from common membership in the community of scholars. Professors do not discriminate against or harass colleagues. They respect and defend the free inquiry of associates. In the exchange of criticism and ideas professors show due respect for the opinions of others. Professors acknowledge academic debt and strive to be objective in their professional judgment of colleagues. Professors accept their share of faculty responsibilities for the governance of their institution.

4. As members of an academic institution, professors seek above all to be effective teachers and scholars. Although professors observe the stated regulations of the institution, provided the regulations do not contravene academic freedom, they maintain their right to criticize and seek revision. Professors give due regard to their paramount responsibilities within their institution in determining the amount and

character of work done outside it. When considering the interruption or termination of their service, professors recognize the effect of their decision upon the program of the institution and give due notice of their intentions.

5. As members of their community, professors have the rights and obligations of other citizens. Professors measure the urgency of these obligations in the light of their responsibilities to their subject, to their students, to their profession, and to their institution. When they speak or act as private persons, they avoid creating the impression of speaking or acting for their college or university. As citizens engaged in a profession that depends upon freedom for its health and integrity, professors have a particular obligation to promote conditions of free inquiry and to further public understanding of academic freedom.

Hiring / Termination Documents

UNIVERSITY OF ILLINOIS
AT URBANA-CHAMPAIGN

Office of the Dean

College of Liberal Arts and Sciences
2090 Lincoln Hall
702 South Wright Street
Urbana, IL 61801-3631

September 27, 2013

CONFIDENTIAL

Professor Steven Salaita
via email salaita@vt.edu

Dear Professor Salaita:

Upon the recommendation of Professor Jodi Byrd, Acting Director of the American Indian Studies, I am pleased to offer you a faculty position in that department at the rank of Associate Professor at an academic year (nine-month) salary of $81,000 paid over twelve months, effective January 01, 2014. This appointment will carry indefinite tenure. This recommendation for appointment is subject to approval by the Board of Trustees of the University of Illinois.

Professor Jodi Byrd will be writing separately to you about your opportunities here, about research support, and about your responsibilities, including teaching assignments.

At the University of Illinois, like at most universities in this country, we subscribe to the principles of academic freedom and tenure laid down by the American Association of University Professors (AAUP). The Statement on Academic Freedom and Tenure of the American Association of University Professors has been since 1940 the foundation document in this country covering the freedoms and obligations of tenure. The AAUP Statement on Professional Ethics is a document of similarly broad application to those in academia. I am enclosing copies of these documents for your information, and commend them to your attention.

We would appreciate learning of your decision by 10/14/2013. I have included an enclosure describing some of the general terms of employment at the University. If you choose to accept our invitation, we would appreciate your returning a photocopy of this letter with the form at the bottom completed and signed. When you arrive on campus, you will be asked to present proof of your citizenship and eligibility to work (see the I-9 form). If you are not a U.S. citizen, this offer will be contingent upon your being able to secure the appropriate visa status. Should you accept our offer, our Office of International Faculty and Staff Affairs is available to assist you with this process.

Please let me express my sincere enthusiasm about your joining us. The University of Illinois at Urbana-Champaign offers a wonderfully supportive community, and it has always taken a high interest in its newcomers. I feel sure that your career can flourish here, and I hope earnestly that you will accept our invitation.

Sincerely,

Brian H. Ross
Interim Dean

Enclosures
c: Jodi Byrd

I accept the above offer of September 27, 2013:

Name: Steven Salaita
Current e-mail address: _____
Birthdate: _____
United States Citizen: _____ Yes _____ No

Signature: _____ Date: _____

UNIVERSITY OF ILLINOIS
AT URBANA-CHAMPAIGN

Office of the Dean

College of Liberal Arts and Sciences
2090 Lincoln Hall
702 South Wright Street
Urbana, IL 61801-3631

Revised October 03, 2013

CONFIDENTIAL

Professor Steven Salaita
via email salaita@vt.edu

Dear Professor Salaita:

Upon the recommendation of Professor Jodi Byrd, Acting Director of the American Indian Studies, I am pleased to offer you a faculty position in that department at the rank of Associate Professor at an academic year (nine-month) salary of $85,000 paid over twelve months, effective January 01, 2014. This appointment will carry indefinite tenure. This recommendation for appointment is subject to approval by the Board of Trustees of the University of Illinois.

Professor Jodi Byrd will be writing separately to you about your opportunities here, about research support, and about your responsibilities, including teaching assignments.

At the University of Illinois, like at most universities in this country, we subscribe to the principles of academic freedom and tenure laid down by the American Association of University Professors (AAUP). The Statement on Academic Freedom and Tenure of the American Association of University Professors has been since 1940 the foundation document in this country covering the freedoms and obligations of tenure. The AAUP Statement on Professional Ethics is a document of similarly broad application to those in academia. I am enclosing copies of these documents for your information, and commend them to your attention.

We would appreciate learning of your decision by 10/14/2013. I have included an enclosure describing some of the general terms of employment at the University. If you choose to accept our invitation, we would appreciate your returning a photocopy of this letter with the form at the bottom completed and signed. When you arrive on campus, you will be asked to present proof of your citizenship and eligibility to work (see the I-9 form). If you are not a U.S. citizen, this offer will be contingent upon your being able to secure the appropriate visa status. Should you accept our offer, our Office of International Faculty and Staff Affairs is available to assist you with this process.

Please let me express my sincere enthusiasm about your joining us. The University of Illinois at Urbana-Champaign offers a wonderfully supportive community, and it has always taken a high interest in its newcomers. I feel sure that your career can flourish here, and I hope earnestly that you will accept our invitation.

Sincerely,

Brian H. Ross
Interim Dean

Enclosures
c: Jodi Byrd

I accept the above offer of October 03, 2013:

Name: Steven Salaita
Current e-mail address: salaita@ut.edu
Birthdate: 9/15/75
United States Citizen: X Yes _____ No

Signature: _____ Date: 10/9/13

University of Illinois
at Urbana–Champaign

American Indian Studies Program
1204 West Nevada Street, MC -138
Urbana, IL 61801-3818

October 3, 2013

Steven Salaita
Department of English, Virginia Tech
323 Shanks Hall (0112)
Blackburg, VA 24061
540-231-7696

Dear Steve:

I'm thrilled to send you this letter to supplement the offer letter you received from Interim Dean Brian Ross last week. This letter outlines some of the additional details of the offer and addresses some specifics about the position in American Indian Studies (AIS).

Interim Dean Ross and the College of Liberal Arts and Science have worked with me to assemble what we hope is a strong and attractive offer. All the core and affiliate faculty in American Indian Studies are truly enthusiastic about your hire, and are looking forward to working with you as soon as you get to campus. We hope this offer demonstrates our real commitment to expanding indigenous studies beyond the North American context, and that it expresses our hope that you will join us as a faculty colleague here at Illinois.

As Interim Dean Ross explained in his letter, you will be appointed at 100% in AIS, at the Associate Professor level with tenure, and with a nine-month annual salary of $85,000. As you will notice, this is increased from the offer letter you initially received, and it is my understanding that the dean's office will send a new offer letter with this updated salary information. If you have not yet received it, you will soon. The university provides annual merit-based raises as an opportunity to increase salary. Resources, such as office equipment, supplies, mailing, telecommunications, and such will be provided by AIS, and ATLAS will provide a computer for your use. Additionally, you will have office space with other AIS faculty. We will, further, offer up to $5000 in moving expenses. At the appropriate time, I will provide more information on contacting movers who contract with the university to offer deeply reduced rates on moving costs.

Your teaching load will be two courses each semester (2/2) with an obligation of four per year. Given that your appointment is 100% in AIS, we will work carefully with you to minimize the number of new courses that you will have to prepare in a given semester as you develop your teaching portfolio at Illinois. In addition, AIS will help balance your service commitments in the unit. We also recognize that you are a scholar in the height of your productivity and that you are working on your next book. To help facilitate your research, we can offer you a two-course release sometime within your first six semesters on campus.

We are also pleased to be able to offer you a startup and discretionary fund package of $10,000 to get you started in your appointment here. The funds will be available in your first semester on campus and may be used for any academic purpose that best supports your work (travel, research assistance, buying books or films, etc.). The funds can be carried forward across fiscal years so that the timing of expenditures may be used to their best advantage for your maximum benefit. Additional research and travel funds may be applied for and secured through application to the university's Research Board which offers funds up to $30,000 to help initiate, bolster, and sustain the research goals of faculty. You can find more information about the available programs and deadlines here: http://crb.research.illinois.edu.

Further, as we have discussed by phone, Illinois has a tremendous number of funds that support faculty research and provide additional course releases (e.g., the Center for Advanced Study, the Humanities Release Time program, the Illinois Program for Research in the Humanities, and the Illinois Mellon fellowships in the humanities program). These funds are open to all faculty to apply for and AIS encourages you to seek out such opportunities to support your work. Our campus also supports faculty research via numerous campus- and college-level programs that routinely benefit AIS faculty even if they are not housed within the department. Thus, you will have some travel support through the campus-level Scholars Travel Fund, which provides tenured faculty members with funding toward one conference per year. Additionally, in recent years, all faculty in the humanities and arts fields—including AIS—have received $1,000 per year in discretionary research funding through the campus's Humanities/Arts Scholarship Support Program (HASS). This will increase to $1,500 this year, and you would be in line to receive research funding from this program as of the 2014-15 academic year. These programs are not housed in our department, and so we do not control them, but I have every confidence that you and other AIS faculty members will continue to benefit from them for the foreseeable future.

Finally, I have begun looking to find a position for your partner through the Dual Career Academic Couples (DCAC) program on campus. This program provides some campus funding to help facilitate partner hiring. While this program does not allow us simply to create new positions on campus, it does serve to incentivize hiring partners where there is a good fit. This can take some time, however, so let me state here that I formally commit to working diligently to find Diana a career path at Illinois that will meet her needs.

I hope you will find this offer attractive. The faculty in the unit are very excited about the possibility of you joining us. American Indian Studies is deeply invested in building a world-class faculty engaged in the global reach of indigenous studies, and we feel you will be integral to achieving that vision. All of us agree that you will make a wonderful addition to our faculty, and we look forward to welcoming you as a colleague and community member of our campus.

Yours sincerely,

Jodi A. Byrd
Acting Director, American Indian Studies

UNIVERSITY OF ILLINOIS
AT URBANA-CHAMPAIGN

Office of the Dean

College of Liberal Arts and Sciences
2090 Lincoln Hall
702 South Wright Street
Urbana, IL 61801-3631

October 09, 2013

Professor Steven Salaita
via email salaita@vt.edu

Dear Professor Salaita:

I am delighted that you chose to accept the offered position with our American Indian Studies Program. This campus has been a wonderful place for faculty and students for a long time. I feel confident that you will find here a good climate for the growth of your career.

I look forward to your arrival on campus and to meeting you at the earliest opportunity.

Sincerely,

Brian H. Ross
Interim Dean

c: Jodi Byrd

UNIVERSITY OF ILLINOIS
Urbana-Champaign • Chicago • Springfield

Office of the Vice President for Academic Affairs
377 Henry Administration Building
506 South Wright Street
Urbana, IL 61801

Christophe Pierre
Vice President

August 1, 2014

PERSONAL AND CONFIDENTIAL

Professor Steven Salaita

via email: salaita@vt.edu

108 Cohee Road
Blacksburg, Virginia 24060

Dept. of English MC 0112
180 Turner Street, NW
Blacksburg, Virginia 24061

Dear Professor Salaita,

As you are aware, on October 3, 2013, Brian H. Ross, Interim Dean of the College of Liberal Arts and Sciences, wrote to you to inform you that Professor Jodi Byrd, Acting Director of American Indian Studies, had recommended you for a position on the faculty of the University of Illinois at Urbana-Champaign. As Dean Ross' letter stated: "This recommendation for appointment is subject to approval by the Board of Trustees of the University of Illinois."

We write to inform you that your appointment will not be recommended for submission to the Board of Trustees in September, and we believe that an affirmative Board vote approving your appointment is unlikely. We therefore will not be in a position to appoint you to the faculty of the University of Illinois at Urbana-Champaign. We write to you today so that you would be aware of this fact and would be able to act accordingly.

Thank you for your interest in and consideration of the University of Illinois.

Sincerely,

Christophe Pierre
Vice President for Academic Affairs

Phyllis M. Wise
Chancellor
University of Illinois at Urbana-Champaign

Urbana • (217) 333-3077 • Fax (217) 244-4770 • E-Mail: chpierre@uillinois.edu
Chicago • 1737 West Polk Street • Chicago, Illinois 60612-7228 • (312) 413-3557

Salon Article and Virginia Tech Response

"NO, THANKS: STOP SAYING 'SUPPORT THE TROOPS'"

First published on August 25, 2013, and
reprinted courtesy of *Salon*.

My 16-month-old son was having a bad day. When he doesn't sleep in the car, he usually points and babbles his approval of all the wonderful things babies notice that completely escape adult attention. On this afternoon, though, he was teething and hungry, a lethal scenario for an energetic youngster strapped into a high-tech seating apparatus (approved and installed, of course, by the state).

When it became clear he couldn't, or wouldn't, sleep it out, my wife and I stopped at a nondescript exit, the kind one finds every six miles in the South, with two gas stations and three abandoned buildings (if you're lucky, you also get a Hampton Inn and Cracker Barrel). While she tended to the baby, I entered a convenience store—one of those squat, glass and plastic rectangles that looks like a Sears & Roebuck erector set—praying it would have something other than beer, cigarettes and beef jerky.

I settled on two Kraft mozzarella sticks, resisting the urge to purchase for myself a shiny red can of Four Loko.

"That'll be $1.82," the lady at the counter cheerily informed me. After I handed her two ones, she asked, "Would you like to donate your change to the troops?" I noticed a jar with "support our troops" taped to it in handwritten ink.

"No, thank you," I answered firmly.

"Well . . . OK, then, sir," she responded in subtle reproach, her smile not quite so ascendant anymore. "You have a good day now."

She had good reason to be disappointed. The vast majority of customers, I imagine, spare a few dimes and pennies for so important a cause. Her response evinced more shock than anger. She wasn't expecting a refusal of 18 cents, even from a guy who looks very much like those responsible for the danger to our troops.

Besides, nobody likes to have their altruism invalidated by a recalcitrant or ungrateful audience.

I could have asked how the donations would be used, but no matter the answer I would have kept my 18 cents. I don't consider patriotism a beneficent force, for it asks us to exhibit loyalty to nation-states that never fully accommodate their entire populations. In recent years I've grown fatigued of appeals on behalf of the troops, which intensify in proportion to the belligerence or potential unpopularity of the imperial adventure du jour.

In addition to donating change to the troops, we are repeatedly impelled to "support our troops" or to "thank our troops." God constantly blesses them. Politicians exalt them. We are warned, "If you can't stand behind our troops, feel free to stand in front of them." One wonders if our troops are the ass-kicking force of P.R. lore or an agglomeration of oversensitive duds and beggars.

Such troop worship is trite and tiresome, but that's not its primary danger. A nation that continuously publicizes appeals to "support our troops" is explicitly asking its citizens not to think. It is the ideal slogan for suppressing the practice of democracy, presented to us in the guise of democratic preservation.

I returned to the car, wondering if it will ever be possible to escape the inveterate branding of war as a civic asset in the United States. My son happily grabbed his snack and giggled as I jingled the change before dropping it into the ashtray.

﹏

The troops are now everywhere. They occupy bases and war zones throughout the Arab world and Central Asia and have permanent presence in dozens of countries. They also occupy every tract of discursive territory in the United States. The troops are our omnipresent, if amorphous, symbols of moral and intellectual austerity.

No televised sporting event escapes celebration of the troops. Networks treat viewers to stars and stripes covering entire football fields, complementing the small-but-always-visible flags the studio hosts sport on their lapels. The national anthem is often accompanied by fighter jets and cannon blasts. Displays of hypermasculine prowess frame the reciprocal virtues of courage and devotion embedded in American war mythology.

Corporate entities are the worst offenders. On flights, troops are offered early boarding and then treated to rounds of applause during the otherwise forgettable safety announcements. Anheuser-Busch recently won the Secretary of Defense Public Service Award and in 2011 "Budweiser paid tribute to America's heroes with a patriotic float in the Rose Parade®." The Army's website has a page dedicated to "Army Friendly Companies"; it is filled with an all-star lineup of the Forbes 500 as well as dozens of regional businesses.

I do not begrudge the troops for availing themselves of any benefits companies choose to offer, nor do I begrudge the companies for offering those benefits. Of greater interest is what the phenomenon of corporate charity for the troops tells us about commercial conduct in an era of compulsory patriotism.

It tells us, first of all, that corporations care far less about the individuals who happen to have served in the military than they do about "the troops" as an exploitable consumer category. Unthinking patriotism, exemplified by support of the troops (however insincere or self-serving), is an asset to the modern business model, not simply for good P.R., but also for the profit it generates.

Multinational corporations have a profound interest in cheerleading for war and in the deification of those sent to execute it. For many of these corporations, the U.S. military is essentially a private army dispatched around the world as needed to protect their investments and to open new markets. Their customers may "support our troops" based on sincere feelings of sympathy or camaraderie, but for the elite the task of an ideal citizenry isn't to analyze or to investigate, but to consume. In order for the citizenry to consume an abundance of products most people don't actually need, it is necessary to interject the spoils of international larceny into the marketplace.

❧

"Support the troops" is the most overused platitude in the United States, but still the most effective for anybody who seeks interpersonal or economic ingratiation. The platitude abounds with significance but lacks the burdens of substance and specificity. It says something apparently apolitical while patrolling for heresy to an inelastic logic. Its only concrete function is to situate users into normative spaces.

Clichés aren't usually meant to be analyzed, but this one illuminates imperialism so succinctly that to think seriously about it is to necessarily assess jingoism, foreign policy, and national identity. The sheer vacuity and inexplicability of the phrase, despite its ubiquity, indicates just how incoherent patriotism is these days.

Who, for instance, are "the troops"? Do they include those safely on bases in Hawaii and Germany? Those guarding and torturing prisoners at Bagram and Guantánamo? The ones who murder people by remote control? The legions of mercenaries in Iraq? The ones I've seen many times in the Arab world acting like an Adam Sandler character? "The troops" traverse vast sociological, geographical, economic and ideological categories. It does neither military personnel nor their fans any good to romanticize them as a singular organism.

And what, exactly, constitutes "support"? Is it financial giving? Affixing a declarative sticker to a car bumper? Posting banalities to Facebook? Clapping when the flight attendant requests applause?

Ultimately, the support we're meant to proffer is ideological. The terms we use to define the troops—freedom-fighters, heroic, courageous—are synecdoche for the romance of American warfare: altruistic, defensive, noble, reluctant, ethical. To support the troops is to accept a particular idea of the American role in the world. It also forces us to pretend that it is a country legitimately interested in equality for all its citizens. Too much evidence to the contrary makes it impossible to accept such an assumption.

In reality, the troops are not actually recipients of any meaningful support. That honor is reserved for the government and its elite constituencies. "Support our troops" entails a tacit injunction that we also support whatever politicians in any given moment deem the national interest. If we understand that "the national interest" is but a metonym for the aspirations of the ruling class, then supporting the troops becomes a counterintuitive, even harmful, gesture.

The government's many appeals to support the troops represent an outsourcing of its responsibility (as with healthcare, education and incarceration). Numerous veterans have returned home to inadequate medical coverage, psychological afflictions, unemployment and increased risk of cancer. The free market and corporate magnanimity are supposed to address these matters, but neither has ever been a viable substitute for the dynamic practices of communal policymaking. A different sort of combat ensues: class warfare, without the consciousness.

As in most areas of the American polity, we pay taxes that favor the private sector, which then refuses to contribute to any sustainable vision of the public good. The only serious welfare programs in the United States benefit the most powerful among us. Individual troops, who are made to preserve and perpetuate this system, rarely enjoy the spoils. The bonanza is reserved for those who exploit the profitability of warfare through the acquisition of foreign resources and the manufacture of weapons.

Supporting the troops is a cheerful surrogate for enabling the friendly dictators, secret operations, torture practices and spying programs that sustain this terrible economy.

᠎᠎

My wife and I often discuss what our son might grow up to accomplish. A consistent area of disagreement is his possible career choice. She can think of few things worse than him one day joining the military (in any capacity), while I would not object to such a decision.

Those who know me might be surprised by my position, but it arises from a belief consistent with my political outlook, that the power of institutions can never overwhelm the simple act of thinking. In other words, even if the military as an institution often does bad things, the individuals that comprise the military do not have to become bad people. Soldiers can certainly be awful human beings, but so can professors, clerks, musicians, executives, landscapers and athletes.

This way of thinking also inversely demystifies the troops, who are burdened with untenable narratives of heroism the vast majority (like those in all professions) do not deserve. I am neither smart nor foolish enough to define "heroism," but I am comfortable saying the mere fact of being a soldier doesn't automatically make one a hero, just as the mere fact of being in prison doesn't necessarily make one evil.

If we recognize that the troops are in fact human beings, then we simultaneously accept that they are too complex to be reduced to patriotic ephemera. Such recognition is unusual, though. People speak frequently of "our troops," highlighting the pronoun as if it is imperative to their sense of national belonging. It is an act of possession that projects fantasies of virtue onto an idealized demographic in the absence of substantive virtuous practices that might otherwise foster national pride. Plutocracy ravages the state; we rebuild it with narratives of glory and selflessness, the troops acting as both the signifier and the signified in this nationalistic uplift.

The selflessness of our troops is particularly sacred. Not only do they bring order and democracy to lesser peoples; they also risk (and sometimes give) their lives for the good of others, so that civilians might continue driving, shopping, dining and watching movies, the hallmarks of American freedom. That these notions of sacrifice connote a Christ-like narrative of individual-death-for-collective-pleasure only endows them with even greater cultural power.

Whether or not our son ever joins the military, questions about the deployment of mythological slogans in the service of socioeconomic iniquity need to be addressed. His joining or not joining will have no effect on that need, which will remain even if he becomes a teacher or doctor. I want him to enter into adulthood in a world where people impeach and diminish the mystification of corporate plunder. More than anything, I want him to participate in the process, whether he does it from a barrack, a cubicle or a corner office.

It would be wise to avoid countervailing slogans, such as the assertive but nonetheless meager Support Our Troops, Bring Them

Home! One goal is to disrupt and rethink, something much easier to accomplish in the absence of shibboleths. Another goal is to continue exploring why support for troops as prescribed by sports leagues and conglomerates actually does a great disservice to the human beings who comprise the military and reinforces a plutocratic imperium for those who do not.

Next time you are asked to "support our troops," then, remember that in a country where wealth decides the fate of so many communities, such an uncritical gesture isn't even worth the change from a broken dollar.

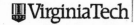

The Office of University Relations
315 Burruss Hall (0229)
Blacksburg, Virginia 24061
540- 231-5396 FAX: 540- 231-1985
email: unirel@vt.edu
www.vt.edu

We have received your note concerning an opinion piece in Salon.com by assistant professor for English, Steven Salaita. Please know that his opinions concerning support for members of the U.S. armed forces in no way represent an official university opinion.

Few universities in the nation support the military like Virginia Tech. The Virginia Tech Corps of Cadets is one of the largest military corps operations among U.S. universities outside the military academies. A larger percentage of our cadets are commissioned into the military than any other school, other than the academies. We rank among our alumni seven U.S. Medal of Honor winners.

Virginia Tech has a V3 certification from Virginia Department of Veteran Services for its hiring of Veterans, the first university in the state to be so designated. Virginia Tech has been recognized by Military Advanced Education as one of America's Top Military-Friendly Colleges and Universities for the 3rd consecutive year. Our work to attract and support veterans has been featured in U.S. News & World Report. We are proud of our veteran students and vets among our employ.

Institutionally and honorably, we support our nation's troops.

However much we may disagree with associate professor Salaita's opinions, we also recognize one of this nation's most cherished liberties ensconced in the first amendment to our nation's constitution and embedded in the principle of academic freedom. He has a right to his opinions just as others have a right to disagree.

While our assistant professor may have a megaphone on salon.com, his opinions not only do not reflect institutional position, we are confident they do not remotely reflect the collective opinion of the greater university community.

Lawrence G. Hincker
Associate Vice President for University Relations
Vietnam era U.S. Navy veteran

Invent the Future

VIRGINIA POLYTECHNIC INSTITUTE AND STATE UNIVERSITY
An equal opportunity, affirmative action institution

INDEX